INCARNATE:
Story Material

ALSO BY THALIA FIELD

Point and Line

INCARNATE:
Story Material

by Thalia Field

A NEW DIRECTIONS BOOK

Book design by Sylvia Frezzolini Severance
Manufactured in the United States of America
New Directions Books are printed on acid-free paper.
First published as New Directions Paperbook 996 in 2004.
Published simultaneously in Canada by Penguin Books Ltd.

Grateful acknowledgment goes to the following journals for printing pieces from this book in earlier forms: *Conjunctions: 37*, "Autobiography (Make a Laundry List of This)"; *Conjunctions: 35*, "Land at Church City"; *The Chicago Review*, "Havoc"; *Facture*, "Incarnate"; *Fence*, "Crewel" and "Story Material"; *How2*, "Zoologic"; *Salt Hill #9*, "Copywrites (Sweat)."

Special thanks to Michelle Ellsworth, Carole Maso, Sherry Mason and Bonnie Metzgar for invaluable creative guidance, and even though these words mean little to them, my boundless gratitude also goes to Lila and Dorje for keeping the heart-world bright within our common kind. —T.F.

Library of Congress Cataloging-in-Publication Data

Field, Thalia, 1966-
Incarnate : story material / by Thalia Field.
     p. cm.
ISBN 0-8112-1599-7 (alk. paper)
I. Title.

PS3556.I398I53 2004
811'.54—dc22   2004011692

New Directions Books are published for James Laughlin
by New Directions Publishing Corporation
80 Eighth Avenue, New York 10011

for Jamie

our assumptions of separateness are unacceptably simplistic,
and we might more closely approximate the facts of existence by
regarding ourselves less as objects than as sets of relationships,
or as processes in time rather than as static forms

Neil Evernden

the clouds will pass, do not try to follow them

Venerable Khandro, Rinpoche

CONTENTS

INCARNATE:
Story Material

Make A Laundry List of This
search
the name of a central character
a weed's dominion   clicks   "all"
search   an overhunted   dependence
this rebuttal, this overmuch   this common content
engine   this overstatement
autocartography
she reads the palm hands down

Make a Hammer of This
                    slow depopulation
one species overtaking its own
search
popular conceptions
flickering   refine searching
even forced across walls of clothing, can't not
find something

a Wake of This
          some splitless spot of calm, can calm against
Make an Excuse of This
domain   enter
the delusion other than intuition; a herd instinct

Make a Ploy of This
a girl   monitors   colors
her slight   conscience
          her miniscule overconsumption
but for clarity, a darker room
the bounded nature of a plane
a perception of cell deaths

some old soft tissue

                            the end of production

the smell of busy bacteria   a grid of sourceless wind

the room manifestly unseen   and windless, wanting

energy   some carbon forms

Make a Point of This

one old wholly [sic] mammoth

she punches, agile   some letters

Make Feedback of This

she enters   an expert

her co-evolving mechanisms

increasing knowledge: poverty, overeating

a verb form slowed to a light speed, caught

        too, well   a self, conscious

Make a Meal of This

portal   some engine

        overinterpreting

        narrower attention

Make a Dance of This

traveling caravan   the drone

of a percent decline

the deepest math   <u>enter</u>

woolly mammoth   or

        in quotations

"thalia field"

Make News of This

mammoth or a mastodon

        relic theory

some decision   to hunt in hunger

the crisis of surviving opulently

        in passing   did not die

Make More of This
                     from one or another
                     slight and constant pressure
one by one by one   the search
in quotations, resulting   in darkness' clear signal

Make A Mockery of This
taken back by Texas Rangers on the spot
enter   "Cynthia Ann Parker"
the result hooded in blood   early American destiny resolves
the history, return

                                    space
the carcass losing useful distinctions
a shape less recognized
Make a Photo of This
overattended   underexistence
a meat substitute   please
the virus spreads by fresh and open holes
an overabundance of overexistence
to overlook what

Make the Most of This
laugh, she the one who reads
confounding results
originally   screens list
clarity, chaotically   the name of the entered
spark   a blink   at the entry exit

Make A Homecooked Meal
Make a Nail of This
breezeless   putsch
        remorse   or graft
generations   supposedly regenerate   the function
the probabilities   turn against   the key
a likely choice   from one to the next

Make Rain of This
name
                    date
a meteor may have hit
Make an Advertisement of This
eminent domain
the three megafauna
whose bones make reasonable evidence
against a single catastrophe theory
the job of extinction   contracted bit by bit

Make a Definition of This
"thalia field"   a quick span of time
aroused   a door at once,   a selfish costume
clothes made to laundry
without weather   fuel   or birth momentum
the work compliant   gains   feeling, DNA
          against this   or the next against   a small overkill
any one edit   just more overattention

Make a Hunt of This
flaw of produce, precious
plastic   a bit of backlight
Make a Fork in the Road
search out hungry for work
the furrow material of spoiled sleep
punching away, a very slow meal
tonight and tomorrow   overextended, species-wise
collecting back pay

Make a Dwelling
a kind of breeze
          from encroaching efforts
our collective areas of detail

she hands over wet clothing
and tools

and thinking
                              back
soft-tissue   a million years of storage

Make a Government of This
restart with a different sort of result
a bride search
a mother
of the last Comanche chief
beyond the pale comes up
takes on a name   in legend, posted
                              walked the continent
myth despite silence
despite the varying powers   of storage
cause ways

land bridges

Make a Fortune of This
mammoth memory
repose   response
in advance of corners, merely tabulations
Make a Traveling Circus
an intended population
some aimless plan, innocent
with incremental growth

Make an Instinct
blank   breezeless   mindless
after it's closed   the door
entices

the hallway
    a rival
    heated by tiny increments
    decreasing songs   boiling over

Make a Video Game
another search
ensuring prisoners and witnesses
separate architecture with separate entrances
Make a Poem
an exit
developers bid   an expensive pitch   for a meal
       a money substitute
the kind fortunes of failure
Make a Microscope
in all walks to tell anything, backward
an unbiased jury with impossible reach
Make a Time Line of This
symbol, punch in
"me," this time   my own   unique supposed
rhetoric overspeaks   the room is quiet but alert
Make a Clock
A Harbor
Make a Gesture
awaiting   ground sloths and armadillos
       the size of tanker trucks
insert   a picture here
a famous reinactment [sic]
of settlers and tribes
a hospitality the size of Texas
       search in quotation marks
hog calling and outhouse races
       "Cynthia Ann"
Make a Mention of This

her festival   and impotence, what breeze
map   what   thinking
     drains   what
river   floods   what   grid
plain   clicks   Texas

Make a Robot of This
or Quanah Parker, for the nine wagons   <u>click</u>
the rifle   his mother's stolen,   a fear fragrance
of flowers   of 1836, a new independence of Texas locked <u>click</u>
a dead silence; Silas Parker

Make a Window
punched in   electric, out

Make a Hand-Woven Fabric
stolen
stolen back
                         what search relieved
taken
taken back
                         a private outfit
Make Progress of This
Make a Meaningful Glance
re-ransomed ironically   an insert
a slow over-hunting

Make a Rhetorical Flourish
of minus numbers
Make a Science of This
Cynthia Ann
lived with the tribe called People
anyway
Make a Plastic Spoon of This

renamed her Naduah
married Peta Nocona with horses and smallpox
what comes up
represents a story in the place of

Make a Lamp
                              scattered, assembled
to keep the flame clear
inseparably you enter   you can't enter it
          or tell me
to enter   "something in quotes"
Make a Beveled Mirror
or a belief   justify this
Make a News Article
afraid   of entering 'myself'
Make a Rational Statement
overfueling   the megafauna may have craved
          this hypothesis, and overgrazed
Make a Theory
an Apology
the herds of necessity
the hunter blooms   one by one
too many skills; too the plug-ins
Make Electricity
and a thousand years'll do the work
the slowing family
          overthinking   underhanded
Make Light of This
easy, moderate overbearing
what looks like procreation hides the truth
numbers incline against time   overworked
handsome   invisible   undertaking
of glacial conditions

Make a Present Instance

Make a Stage Play
at the junction of a U.S. Highway and Farm Road 262
Thalia field
Make an Unbearable Certainty of This
collapse   winsome
shoal   exact
immobile   mammoth
metaphor   sloth
fake   skins
          wrong means
Make a Whole [sic] Mammoth
this something, different   each subtraction
                    a slow accrual
the name changed
Make a Hard Knock
a turbulence too stable   new industry, weeds
where Thalia field, Texas   would not so much fail
as provide some rich habitat, some production

Make Shit of This
failing
this marginal accident, overgrown
renewal of a tenacious breed
the settling   of names   punched, proceeding
where "thalia field" and any related sites

Make a Supermarket
fall out of the darkness   into obscurity
Make a Cardboard Box
originally named Paradise, until the post office rejected that
for Thalia itself
make a left at the creek, Thalia field lies to the south

Make a Wanted Poster
survey available
futile   lead to
the manifest apparition of abundant life
Make a Scrapbook of This
a place plotted in 1910
Thalia field wasn't drilled until 1925
Make an Ink Pen
an oasis   a museum basement
Make a Fence of This
becalming decomposition
                    writing more and more
and nothing new under the sun
with a long-abandoned school, Thalia's deserted houses
and decaying businesses cast grim foreshadows

Make a Decision
this carcass, feet from finding it
Make a U-Turn
feet from forever ending
a prairie which appears without finish, the sentence deserted
this dark room   clear and quiet and quite breezeless
                    an underproducing reserve
of willing   unforgiving   dependance

Make a Fuel Economy
on refining searches
and power flows out of the system
an opening   an engine
        deep
                    ends
Make a Roll of Tape
result   in habit
without quotation

Make an Oil Painting
whose borders move
with annual rainfall of 23.9 inches
grazed first and fenced
the loamy land between sand rivers
once contained some herds
Make a Promise of This
        that first drill   the results   barbed
        ranch building, the namesake
        near Paradise, the high school closed
                but at its heyday produced 50,000 barrels of crude
                    as the interstate intersects County 6
Make a Drive-In Movie
the result of autobiographical plateau
abundant and empty
Thalia field
devastated by tornado
for many seasons an economic overevent
        resigned to remain fallow
        until Thalia field nationally
                rebounds as a major helium reserve in the 1950's
Make a Delayed Reaction of This
        onions and oil and sweet potato
        bales of cotton and bushels
        of wheat and sorghum
        wild fruits fed the tribes, the buffalo road
accidental   to what appears   tangential
to know   the old dovetail
                              the cow skull still
one step behind time   measured   between contacts

Make a Note of This
may 4, or 5th in Crowell, the Cynthia Ann Parker Festival
celebrated in the area where she disappeared

Make a Plot of This
outhouse races instead of Kiowa bands
      the richness of hog calling   home, forced
      from her days with little Quanah Parker
lost child and husband
enter Thalia field
depopulated   the area   slides
     back   revealing the moves

Make a Long Story Short
by keyword
one carcass and a billion bacteria
"Down the road, Thalia, population 104, is almost a ghost town"
a consumer history   for all to find
how much I eat   the calculations show
the post office closed
Cynthia Ann
and Helium   production but no grocery
    protected
Thalia field from the open
range   some raid, some captive
    taken back
Make a Baseball Bat
harvesting wind
Make a Bridge
A Basket
to search products for further uses
against a background of energy
skins and food   a Giant Sloth
Make an Abstract Noun
as consumption of nonrenewable resources grows
even at tiny imperceptible percents
then 10,000 years' supply of oil will last only 125

Make an Equation
the oil leases on Thalia field since 1901
                              produce think
produce
                    think

Make a Bicycle
three-inch pipeline reserves
to the railway at Foard City
dip and   exponential functions
Make a Common House Fly
replace overhunted mastodons
in the plain, the math because it's late
Cynthia Ann was only nine
with electronic memories, raid again
production dropped to 20,000 barrels in 1948, and stays
in a trap, writing
"the young people are moving away"

Make a Wool Hat of This
drilling Thalia field for nothing
Make a Dog Collar
an Escalator   the hardest places
Make a Pair of Handcuffs
collapse neat extinctions
Make a Television Sitcom   strange coincidences
named for the flower or for nothing
mines and ranches, new settlers musing
over millenniums barely clearing the hill
          as laundry rooms happen

Make a Mountain or a Mole Hill
rich land for other riches
think clearly

                    the mastodons happened
nicely
Make a Hair Salon
at   33°59'5" N
            99°32'15" W   to eke out value
            at some expense
enter or ambush
"Cynthia Ann Parker" called back
a search for herself
a festival, a hog call   a missed breath
the quantity behaves a certain way   in the story
whose rate of searching is proportional to its size
there isn't anything to it
the exponential function describes
any or mass extinctions
Make a Drum of This
skin, intestines stretched, or hide
fenced in or out
skim the collective overbiography
and circle back for comfort, slowly
Make a Warm Meal
Make a Clothes Line
            enter in the exit

the *first*   dispersed
then nothing   there was no face
but iron filings and handfuls of nails
spilled in bloodied labor, a mother's pit
put back,   wanting nothing but body
tacks, broken glass, splintering plywood, nettles
rosethorns   (spirit who had badly chosen)   (a child)
stuffed   Why?   with oneself   rubble of a house
(one who is recognized) (the walls stick) (the yellow light)   the throat
corrupted   legs split across a bed   (slide into the kitchen unheard)
where parents suffer   (complicated)
(adored)   (their armors)   they adored their *second*   later
(moved their lips) unconscious   rowboats wobbling)
their senseless newspapers, teased
some kind of nosebleed (she's sent with a rag)
blurry light   biting bread   not darting up
Later   (a pinching motion)   a *third*
(at the school   (always scrubbing   (evolving patterns)
a door half shuts)   class perceives   (sharpeners
(teachers warn   there is a light, (deeply green
"go to the next room"   (tall and too thin)   signals a chum (looks down)
embarrassed) (homeless)   (a stench)   evokes   skulls
the room exposed   quicksand   afterbirth
some biological   vestigial   government
(tumbling)   into quicksand (some antidote)   a red staircase (one, plus)
(one) addition, gaping   (broomhandle slides down the wall)
makes the milk bottles crash
So   the *fourth* jumps   (born in snow)   she walks the town
yellow in the puddles   (free as a joke)   and the sun's empty
in empty clouds)   and there's nothing in the street but her truancy
to sculpt   (a test tube) fleshy   her coat drags the slush

they lock up   spirited crows   (she heard)
        churning (sounds)   river barges quick   (hangings)
      followed by drownings   chattering (cremating   (teeth)
                    tongue dry (cold)   lick
              down the brick steps to the river, one two languages
(and yet somehow)   a *fifth* regretful
passenger   arrives   (at court   bruised (queen)   of the feet) parade
      breaks (an overrun hallway   (she notices   (thousands of mice
        lace-like)   dirty floors)   awash
          a rolling tide of ears and tails   sloshing back and forth
          somebody   (bright blue)   a suit (at the other end
          ripe with arms and children's share   where the foot falls
          shiny orange eyes in a wondrous flat face   (whistles)
      sees her (him? suddenly)   nowhere   (up close)
                  is it really? and notice   irises softening like chocolate
melting rush (of warmth   (a sip peach syrup   they enter an office
      she (he?   lifts her to a very tall stool   and whistles (damply
        through gloved fingers the mice (every corner (of the room, retreat
he (she?   closes the door   and a newspaper

        a day goes a day she does not every day
        the day she gave   (away) a day

)(clip burns up)   a firecracker (a fat) old   parent
        kissing can't stop squirming he was laughing   and choosing another
                            (her writing) hand)
a *sixth*   spits   a different color   smudging
                  (the stool)   against (one against one) the floor
(he's laughing   white and clear
                  "so see here" (gloves feel her hair)
(winking "we'll take you" out of this")   a finger
            lingering on the desk   (a hot knife (slides up butter)
                  "there is one" place"   a *seventh*
            (out the window   (a) small (metal box)

(with ruby knobs)   maple?   and a glow of violet) drifts the snowbanks)
    (the box wears a three pointed napkin) pointing to the window (the rats)
coercing the town   for bread   every turret on the bridges crawling
        (and pale buildings forecast)) (a   (a)   foreigner
("there won't be any" remaining")   (here"   in gold   in maple
        I'll be married to an unknown man   (his no color hair)
                                by nightfall s/he meant
an *eighth* approaching "if you're starved" (for a familiar dinner, she meant)
                    pointing   "Just go inside the box"
"be safe" (safe) safe (she kept saying)   <u>safe</u>   safe
            SAFE
(without stepping in it)   the metal sides around her
        (I, too big in it)   satin) soft rubies   (on the handles
        (but no handles))   just a tiny heart (in a bottle) on the
    pearl inlay   coffin (pocked with alabaster)   buttons)
    (and the lid puckered silk)   and realized   (hungry)
    it stinks   (not joking)   it was
            (joking   (private)   (*ninth*)

        in the hospital mother doctors said caused by one or caused by some
        related causal complication; the mother says names, heard armies
        causing the caused by her, had not handled signs strongly, to intervene
        afterward though if unarmed the doctors think what if we'd not

    tenth   (began)   )(soon enough
    just in case   (there would be   a struggle   (private)
the *eleventh*   (bearing midnight   slide (scalded)
into bed   her cold dissolving   in sheets (but rather) sits   backward)
(in the chair at her tiny desk)   in this way (she sees   a *twelfth* (alive)
(at the mattress, enraged   (shredding)   bedclothes for a body
(to rip into; the zombie)   corpse without   a will, animated)
        for good or (evil mechanically) enacting (the bidding master
        (a flesh and blood robot) (needing neither) food nor rest, toiling
    endlessly without   (complaint   wavering)
    (information recorded   (separately)   another page

(rip)   disrupting   (noisily)   all the branches of family
          zombie of potions   (dinners)   and spells (love) to keep it "up"
thirteen   in a flash (speaks (a rush) of colors (feeling (borrowed books)
(possessed her)   and she spoke   (electronically   (from one:

    a young supposed to years later some displaced neighbors
    and though the child walked rigid and bore no expression
    convinced who she was, her empty grave, her cry, exile the body,
    the letter marks in the pine, some Hell keeping her infallibly
    in the flock

the *fourteenth*   (swiftly) diary (empty)   (some phone numbers)
              and a doodle of a house shape (or rat)   (by hand)
     (more pages)   handwritten   *(fifteenth)*   rumpled in a dress pocket
          (the hammering-sickness)   decades later
     (the glass of grenadine (she knew it was)   (hammering)
 (the capital split in two, one half crushing) the waiting) nightgowns
          feet (having molded) (conceived)   again   the songs were gorgeous
     the hospital sank (below sea-level   (the snow   most of the records
          (the symptoms) didn't travel
          to breakfast (she can smell)   (drunken soldiers)
(words) or her parents taken (to the railway station, school) (their cares, laps
  laughs) their silhouettes)   at the table   (still chatting)
          and the *sixteenth* lingers   (seeing steps)   breath)
     (the women marrying wrong men in huge ceremonies) (outside)   again
          (in twenty-one sensations)   invisible   (plus one)
                    (piece)   skin caught up with enormous snow
     sewage   (seeps into cathedrals, stone floors shine in the wind puzzle
(her face) jarred) repairs (the wars)   (vague memories) circle
(the *seventeenth*) feeling (a new draft)   smiling   (adamantine)
     jigsaw pieces in blood (soap shavings) and seeds)
          blowing across ice (give up the parents
  with telephone wire) (write on them) (two more, two soldiers, *eighteenth*
nineteenth))   spread for winter (vermin and) *twentieth* (she might)
grow taller   grow smaller

(after human)   (biography)   to be (safe)   <u>safe</u>
                              SAFE (safe(the sound the snow plays(locking
layer upon layer)   book jacket compartments (behind walls) girls) stand
     in   completeness   solid,solid   house
                    however many (every)   minute (sensing)   counts
(history) they found)   *twenty-first*   and no progress
not without a bruise   (a new machine)   a left-hand)   (scrawling
     just enough justice to account (any source)   less)   one)
faded years   later   unrecouped flight recorders
(armies rape enemy women) (and flock) as a body count (as though they did)
what heaps these aggregates delude   (as aggregates)   families, their
                                        colors (laugh)
   at what understatements allow) ((a long series of ones)
                         making every number
         (born   reborn   assuring   (irrational)   promises
   like   understanding one   plus   one, or   "there is nothing" (we want)
   (wrong)   with precious birth

From the house, hills descended on three sides by road

> hills road and steep. She lived in the meadow, character-cleared and mud. Mud made the mountain shaky and still when she gazed out the character-door at the clearing, the mud, and the mountain back behind, how old and how glass she is.

That is, behind her the mountain as usual, but before her the glass door and mud and no memory

> taken in and a deep breath and a large glass of water downed to the eye-sockets, to the pocked eye sight through the bottom of the glass. Old is memory when it does not character up. Image is all memory or grass. How she scenes and not one. And so the mud sets up, meadow shakes, grassless mountain high behind, and the three steep roads from the house downhill.

When the sun unchecks and the shadow beneath your arm melts.
When the water is too big for you and you're plastic impeachable.
When the fever in the moon swells the last frogs.

And somewhere on the horizon a Man-of-action cut out puppeted from where actions are sewn nearly together. Man-of-action's hunger is prodigious after action. The strings which hang him hang him perilously moving. He's more a cut-out after the action of feeling. Only the horizon where he plans his outs beats his heart like a young broken horse

> but a horizon is so nearly never out as a cut; everyone knows a horizon is only hungry, and every string dangles someplace temporarily while the puppet is barely really. Man-of-action makes a tiny caption of a boat tipping rarely and perfectly. His perfection strings danger

or hunger after a sidekick's equal action. Hungry, he is led to any plate and disburses himself gladly, captive to the action of sweetness' cut: a voracious web, scened with insatiable character. All lines, all motivation, all movie. Toward the horizon he puts his look where he barely nearly road off but keeps remembering that he did.

When skin gets wet to the touch and the ancient stones stand up.
When cold is alternated quickly with warmth at the bottom of the alphabet.
When you've slowed to an attic of quotations.

And so forth the hero attaches according to the law of Similars

with boat-horse or army he captions the mountain non-acting in heavy sunlight; hard dew moistening his lip as old as the Catskills, but clean. He puts himself in courses of like-curing-like curing everything he might be found making
"between curl and contraction" his likeness when action meets completing all the necessary and muscular actions planning. Quietly is not action as the hero armors up a planless devastation of torsos in glass motion without complicated glass motions. Character fills his moves as a scene evaporates to dew strings twisting in the managed accelerating of his heart rate.

With this in mind, stands meadow and mud just the scene's effort, minding where she sits, a sight of the horizon cut down by the hills road steep. Now young old might be found arguing the house or a mind made up of mud, drying where grass pokes through final scattered hay. What would a mind do if it captured an act wondering what to make of it or nothing?

The glass door and glass through which she takes pictures stands open where she stands motion open. Old is the down by three roads mud and shaky, character steep, and mud-images she could keep string warm. Today there may be wetness to the standing and an atmospheric pressure without a trace of cloud. Dew is the magic sweat of the world, or the bad word she looks virgin upon. Sun as the mind packs hay, meadows firm up the fallen mountain doorway.

Perhaps after leave-taking the open road, taking leave of her sense of her ageless old home, perhaps-or-perhaps, or never to return up the three roads steeply down. All three are ancient songs forgotten on the Hudson: one for things she can't do; one for things she can't undo; one undone completely.

When mist enters the frenzy of firewood and ignites the changing.
When one ash path forestalls the progress of the flame path.
When downhill is the short amnesia of double-handed string words.

from a hovering point over the red clay path (a lane dusted with blistering) her eyes follow him on stages teetering, her wings that is, wet and not quite conscious, his wings really hands playing forward into the past fretted grabable; a there tense ensemble past tense, forward of it, pushing into a path he's grasping: all neck, all keys, into hymn.

at last but faithfully abominable. Her eyes make tiny dervishes on the parched silence, fully parted to let loose a vowel slack in overexposed noon, scratching at opened seeds (he lands without prints for her) so that neither dares count prints, or lay them to lip in seasoned glare. His dance a pilgrim of patterns glaring too holy to mistake for mistakes.

a billboard becomes Seraph the highest angel six, whole wings of calendars open, one for each day fluttering the rocky lane like anything red, like anything she can say mistakes are like, though he's the red one.

one mounting. One receiving. A bird forgives the beating up the entrance, as he could pardon the mention of the seventh missing day. This time holy places gather in permanent redemptions up the canyon turned off from familiar. No amenities. No public utilities. The population is bliss freak, and church.

the town above hangs for him now above, and slightly high that way. High an ordinance of loss. High an anticipated beforehand. High the genetic unfinishable. High the deepest kissed past tense. Roof of unapproachable fire escapes. That nest of churches, for lack of a better word, huddles high in his sight, on its undamnable burning seat, and hers way behind and tipping.

it is left for her to hover atheist and downward glancing. Not a single communion broached with binoculars loaded. Were eagles approaching a mile, a mouse might collapse to a print. But her wings bulk in balancing itchy devotion to whatever, in doctrinal whereby. Feathers aren't muscles, yet oiled for repelling a rain not coming for nine hundred ninety-nine miles or years; same thing, she thinks, same thing.

and below her his knees at the gate lips of ground meet kissing. Avenue the churches or blocks and street churches, for lack of a better word, every structure a church, every never his heart repelling tourists of grace for his soon expiation, turning back a cherub, second order angel on a self-same map, a winged child mispronounced.

out of stairs he could dispense his own suffering. Churches, for lack of a better word, bow upright to foundations set to poverty, to lift of thrice-born melancholy. One coupon of atmosphere, a bountiful vulture. How a town consumes with lacking better words than churches, yet only consumes churches. Welcome the hagiography of reflected celebrity.

his head lifts to the altar, for lack of a better word, another rumored virgin, what he's lost the chorus sacrificed, losing denomination in their say-so. Churches, for lack of a better word, fake the orange cones at detours consummating. Welcome to your very raptured transience of patterning. Each church re-animates eternity for a slim visitation.

once he gains, for lack of a better word, a body's drunken messenger, wax-wings instantly fathered, his better word falls toward offering. Tar-stained hands fly stones at one heat unimpeachable. Dust red prints wait in the tense of his tentative printing. Still high and hungry, one afflatus a scalding sunlight numb despite excessive longing. Each sweet translation of relics, cloaked in stained glass, balances skeletons before his each translation tarnishes the last translation. These sentences reflect attachments and wide glances from a sky profane of blue, as blank of believing in churches as his city is full. She believes in them on his behalf from a clueless, senseless perch.

sacred aims at blood detachment contain mortal layers of systems. Sins patched of pine tar, mosses which don't mind this rain. Plant the animal

kingdom, or any small landing. Cycling bundled roots congest with
slippery stasis; an alibi lane in the depth contraption.

but high up in Church Town, for lack of a better name, a stage looses
shadows inside the mission, a town unwieldy with churches, for lack of a
better word, burdened with them and yet undeniably justified. Shadows
and temperatures take umbrage in the testament, kneel beside dusty jubes,
rolling beneath carved pews, his attention clots for shadows faithful to
permanent dwellings.

his feet are likely and pious approaching scriptured ongoings. His ongoings
unblamable statuary, the furnishing of flesh made undiseased. Flight as she
thinks her sanctuary in motion, digging from wings into a small repeated
phrase, trembling at his faith.

or put one last way: without these churches, for lack of a better word, many
denominations force face to city landings; wingspans irrelevant or wholly
threaded, he would fret away the last full upholding, undo his full-blooded
erection, wait: there could be another annunciation, interrupting flight.

invisible blanks hold the doors open double and barely parted, but do part
upon curious muscles. One body makes a street a multitude of church
buildings: assemblies and abbeys, apses and mihrabs, cathedrals mandiras
monasteries chapels stupas temples; he is aching in worship, and with hands
that strive to forgive the height of churches, for lack of any word for faith
in height, or what passes unending, she hovers.

in general, take the bags off
skin them first, empty of muscle tone
tenacity or fat, the ability to take orders, independently detach them
they're always heavy when they start
with water and membranes and chapters barely visible to outside eyes.

the bags, for a start, were legs once
but now the cells are loose and open, giving themselves room
for growing, giving themselves flushing out, water moving
like a river through a baggie, salmon pounding against rocks
a burlesque of questions, rapidly, their skin soaked and ripping off the bone.

the envelope contains what she wanted to say, starting as a phrase probably
only the tiny word, "hi" or "I" or "I'm" or "you're," something along that line
something as small as a drop of water on burning rock. The word small
and the envelope enormous and the word has room to roll in the bottom
snagging in the creases, evaporate or get lost.

he gets home and sees a stranger futzing, lingering with the envelope
arranging the word so it looks smaller than it is; a word like "or" or "yes"
or else "no" or "sure." Some small word he might pull from the bottom
of the medium-sized envelope labeled "so far" or "maybe," three weeks old
a very medium-sized envelope not yet made of skin.

so the cells are still, as you can imagine, shapely. They cling perhaps:
their original integrity, function, I think, not knowing much about cells
but that healthy they travel in shape and size constantly up rivers, piling up
here and there, but laughing, bottlenecking like envelopes, in a surge
of playfulness through post offices.

but panic spews bags detached and emptied, muscles stiffening
drawstrings on the envelopes, the bags long stockings of legs, taking more
water, or in this case, the little word starts stuttering, attaching itself, not
for meaning, but perhaps to fill its cells, to others, bringing them over
like one brings up mouthfuls.

the envelope becomes what can realistically be called a bag, within hours of
opening, the binge of words, now in longer clusters, but clusters
and invisibility move at odds, to say the least, with clustering trying meaning
the words losing self-effacing habits — words which start as giving, she pours
what she could possibly think, little by little into the legs

whatever, the skin envelope, which takes on bulky shapes of following
thoughts, "oh yea" she adds, for a binge of openness she gorges on, delaying
rest, the bag binged and filling emptily of all that's ever empty, every gift
a sea-signal, narrowly repeating some recollected rush of ocean, "helped"
a longed-for getting, a slow, painful, elaborated

starvation of salmon on the return, there will be no counter-effect, knowing
the monstrousness of binging bags like weirs catch envelopes; eagle-eyes
assume a fatal ending, when cells deform — letters beat each other
past recognition, battle upstream where no dictionary could admit them
grown grotesquely long, jaws distorted, hooked teeth gash on rock

renounced — a stutter of unchecked synonyms, expressing symptoms
full to bursting, the body, legless, still leaking, exhausts itself, brings
one bag to completion, finally to some waiting house, at some odd hour
to the doorstep like a corpse in his absence;
a crime committed in the unspelled name of nothing, the name of a river

the name of fish she only knows by stammering
one dreary hope she's outpouring, swallowing steps
the sound of a baggie in the river being cleaned, water shreds plastic
salmon falling up to meet salmon coming apart, home to a gift
enveloped in sympathy, exhausted by their sacrifice

— a glimpse she can't dump enough trash over, or catch
too few pebbles along the shore, the words should he take them, far ahead
in a bag reversed, the head of a stream — a sample of "okay" or "oh"
spawning a vague purpose, a vengeful puke of rebirth — extinction surplus.

What did he mean

      when he said "zoo," when he said, "zoo reality is much softer," or was it simply "softer"? What did he mean when he said the zoo was a much softer place "than a palace," that the zoo was softer than a palace and we were the "palace pets"? What was he spelling when he broke brute silence and said we were nothing but pets "sunk in softness"?

What did that man mean, that man, mean as he was, mean to say

      with that baby swaddled, with that intimate frown, mean when he said, "that zoo is nothing," as though he could continue to connote that the zoo was nothing "more than a pillow," or really he meant a cruel assessment: that the zoo is nothing more than a pillow's "softness," that softness being "something these animals seem to sink into." What aim his drifting arrow took, his suggestive fingers curled around the rough wool of his senseless baby.

He was bored in captivity, this mean man who came to mean much more to us than he could have when he expressed himself outside our cages "with child"

      and us, expecting a mean onlooker as they all are in the particular fate we've come to call onlookers, and what they've come to mean: to come and stand. But this one was meaner and we looked at his involvement, "great" with child and coming from someplace "rocky," evidently not "cushioned," not a palace where he could pet something. He onlooked for a while longer and proposed himself to us, which we weren't sure meant "flocculent" or perhaps "plaint," but in neither case was it a just import. He was just plain lost in what he really meant, and wanted us to mean it too.

Then we noticed another onlooker looking on, this time to this "child-bearing" man rather than to us, doubling our own looking in an unexpected layer so that we were all there extracting meaning from this native man & baby

> bred into a version of a mean man, prickly as they come when they've been bored in captivity, when they've lost their wild dream which they do perpetually when they dream "as a sign of loneliness." When they dream their loneliness and call it "softness" and conjure up all he can feel "about his own self-hating hating."

If he weren't so self-hardened could we help him say what he means, rather, he remains before our various cages, saying nothing more than what he means when he thinks, "this zoo is so soft," or "what I wouldn't give for a taste of that effortless." That effortless lie hissing out his lips, "time without end"

> as much to his tiny infant as to time without obligation he thinks we mean.

Should we suggest the baby go first, to the dry concrete moat, to the piss-reeking "pillow" like a "pillow does"? We mean it when we say "captivity makes us mean" and when we repeat to him that captivity makes one mean "more than anyone watching," or mean "as a stung bull," both. The baby is what we mean when we walk back and forth like that

> his eyes golden with decisions about the pacing mean; his smallest step resounds in the chiseled fibrous rock of our habitat. Drop the baby man we mean when we think "softness is a value of death, prison, or poisoned time," and we don't mean to bring up softness as a value of escape.

Drop the captive baby.
Drop the not yet mean or meaningful baby and drop the meaning of baby.
Drop the mean and debased watching and
Drop meaning nothing in that jumping tongue.
Drop the baby so the other man can really mean it when he says,
"I would go to the zoo but I just can't stand the animals"

In privacy, there are spots and thoughts. The sun, the broadcast star (old organizing principle) casts shadows on an earth transmitting — the box as a whole excepted in a gesture for the unrepaired. The private eye sits dark. Grey on grey, the curving surface offers itself, each face-point invisible during the population. The boy, large and mute, is better off; lids down, his umbra gruesome, a corpse glow-hum (the detective imagines) on all the unopened channels. He drags a sad plug whose extension reaches no wall, no ghost; he can't muster revenge, finding no outlet there. Dark hail and whims across his face, with colors secret only the simulcast undetected. Stories of children take place where electricity hits ground, until impact shatters mere obstacles into burnt extremes. But the off of grey is his best black, even on, "pure black" his missing hoax of chromatism; a life's dried blood. There are increasing heiroglyphs in his box, split shadows, forensic kinship, and airwaves slack as string, don't forget, windless fancy and a father replaying all afternoon: a tall glass of scotch, the first spots in his glassy eye, a mottled reception of the perfect present . . . *he's moved; he's fallen.*

line after line creep up toward him as the snow-static gets deeper in the surface

the televised blinks some unconscious formation, a narcoleptic broadcast of egos as the boy receives a future channeled on and off in relative light. Drunk, the patched detective solicits current: who was where when and how what's always happening: a sharp avenging kidnap. Thousands of hands on his remotest thought. The boy (on or off) was given to him nine months afterward as a gift. All absences grasped, dead air on a dead box, dense dead wood framing a colorless maternal desperation, a despondent menu, mediocre normalcy, and the nearest horizon an after-

grey glow, a greenish thrill on the frontal cortex. The transparent sus-
pects eclipse to grey as the memory (the thought) collapses without
power. "To be wise, a man needs know only how to steal," his thought
(memory) crackles misread, his private eye looming toward the
unpocked face of the boy, shades of silicon curving in his dry and watery
reflection. He recalls what his mistakes have in common: the viewer a
manufactured convenience. All ten-inch figures pale in this lift-off of
greasy plastic, a smoke-stained appliance the old way, a box blinking, he
smacks it hard — and the room falls freer of light, his nuptial time-zone.
He's alone and true enough. Children these days, he thinks. Sun kills
them through their heads. By the day-cradle the detective hoses down
the heartburn, whiskey a small news-puddle around the child's advertised
loss of perspective. A breast nothing but the stone of a Saturday plat-
form. But in the evening, a single bulb. If you don't change, he remem-
bers, you die. "When I'm famous . . . " his boy said, "but not before."
The detective squinted at him until his tenth birthday, the old mother in
the boy an echoing entertainment, dead and changing. Even beyond the
surge of thoughts, motile with his memory schedule, he sees no differ-
ence in change or resistance to change; on or off, the eye functions hys-
terically. The detective feels her hole in his wall, an imperfection the
child couldn't inherit. He thinks (remembers) the boy's fingers spasming
by his side as though ripped with an undeliverable charge. That is what
private eyes thieve from the city utility. In fact, until the woken box, the
air had appeared so empty. But a flick of finger and honeymoons upfill a
sweet Bacchanal of doll-bodies. "Who are all these people?" the father
asks. "Our family," the boy snaps. A generation instantly bored. The
parade morphs to a glyph, his large eye zipping to a blink. "What have
you been doing since the last time you were who you aren't," he gawks.
The boy is grey, the box is grey, boys and boxes pass for grey in the cos-
metic "is" of their disguised "isn't." "Yet," he thinks, "I can't help it."
Life being mostly a matter of disagreements about energy, both parties
refuse to correct their birth defects. Yet somehow the detective is father
to this circle, defective agitator of pure miracle.

hope   like fear
the personality premise   to overcome
saying 44,435,556 names   desperate for cure
or others to cast us back, casting around
a spell, a bruised lock   beads around the yarn
express   disenchanted habits of yearning
jail   for each convicted body   stone flesh, iron links
imprisoned on a trestle bridge perch with every sign of locomotion
    and nothing coming of it
        (once spoken: no trains, none are
          but all are: trains)
hung to the big house, hung up, hanging out every moment
tracks reflect a river below, one still grows   nauseous of the whistle
    as dirt trails from pant legs
across the dusty yard,   scars so dark even sunlight can't find them
    secreted of shadows illegible with conviction
    cell walls fingered   a cool place between rocks
        where no slug would naturally root
      picturing a hole into a tunnel into a cave into nowhere
      half-lit physical mouths and arms grasping
unlike a turned sleeping back, not warmth, not human, not even once
solitary confinement mercy to the light switch, to what they let you picture
    for the moments when a mind opens,   a back softening

because no one personally sees prisoners   signal eyes crossed
    and spoken they won't be heard, in other words, one sentence
    none are speaking and none aren't   fools' hands uncoupling
      disease   some train of manners derailed, their disease
      ah shucks or second thoughts these bars (looking out and in at once)
        remorseful at whatever horrid act   too random, too ignorant
    a fit of terrible freedom, samsaric glitch   some act, word, some

reckless thought, grabbed
        some marching band that didn't kick off
        some attachment to plot, some photographer darkening
        the "perfect day for this or that"   with filters
"the future" and "commitment" sharing an equal enthusiasm
     for getting fucked over
     the way the imagination fires too much hope on the calendar
how the brain stem just fires for the hell of it, the mind catching up
makes some sense of the picture, translated can't fit with the outside world
    transmitted, they can't explain   the dream
        what it was they only meant to say
sun composting careless verbiage, haphazard waste by the end
a good mixture of artifacts collects in the lens, one hopes they'll come out nicely
    like food labels label what's edible
    the shit comes later, proof   positives   of what went in
    after hours in emulsion   and urine tests   coercions packaged
    colorfully   canteens dealing ambivalent currency   a few common fears
     and the tracks make sense in the yard outside, a few scars
    the devil by the Vatican   reaffirmed   his work-effects
        giving us more room in the big house alone
once spoken   this life is over   it is more bad sense   our patronage taxed
  using up the rotted surplus the government foods doing out time in the prison
        open

           parenthesis
      (meanwhile)
        mud models itself after a late day thunderstorm
        forming to the foot
after the muscles it takes to speak around the sharp blade, a documentary
       there hasn't been a grass seed here in half a century
    even birds don't bother   possessed
the skill to turn around in narrow corners, in razor wire
or down the cafeteria line with a tray, gaining strength   eye-contact
        the good face one works without mirrors

eat our words when nothing else tastes natural, and then alone on the cot later
        nothing returns like stray memory where it's fed, locked out
to have played with toys when they said to
          either you're in or   (no matter)
          how long you've been filing down the bars you're in
                                until you're not
   the full expanse   no one passes the cloister without a curse
          the space of a cell, its perfect release
     somehow the love of god forsakes the fist, it could open they forget
more easily in the mind   the first weapons of love-making
                are often the sharp truths in soft food
    so redeem them and invoke some Demons, suddenly believed-in
          which must be spoken Name by Name
          each Subject in his rightful seat
            this Infernal Monarchy called out — Past!
whatever archangel made the hell of living memory
                  of each fuck-up of personality
          in order of our very right reasons
          for all that is wrong, a spell without excuse
          using the letters in all the right order
              but mixed beyond sense, perverse
   because all that is wrong are the devil's various duties
     mispronounced   these horrible hours when Intuition
once the bright dew of the meadow
a sparkling teenage girl, our intuition, she's possessed,
                turns out
    beds disturbing men whose fingers nothing touches
      except her night   spoken that she wouldn't return
she hasn't   and the scrapes and cuts
she was not really one of them, only walking bloodless
          one of ours   can't heal properly
             that Intuition must win or die quietly
on the river stones, instincts which make some animals godly
and some try to run into the other exit, fail against it
         exorcising the fertile option in a land made muddy

stony and reversed

our one last orgasm, remembering her flesh and the smell

of her breath   until Beelzebub the emperor of the legion

of wrong notions hears his moniker and the Seven Kingdoms

of Bad Ideas which follow:

Sense — Impulses — Hope — Doing Something —

Holding — Ascendancy — Disappointment — Fear

these rule the religions of heaven

name each in their early waking, our cold slick hands denounce

the 23 dukes, 10 counts, 11 presidents and 100 knights

each with some good answer to the evidence of action

go on and see which train's coming

tormented souls in the rising doused out, hastily

better off doused out

in heaven's immediate hell we've only just begun the night's scratching

our fingers migrate   on concrete layers of skin each with a name

turns take an hour round the whole floor

one each of the 6666 legions, each comprised of 6666 devils

making altogether 44,435,556 different devils to be shouted out

each in its order, careful

one mistake ignites other beginnings   wasted

spell   shattered   the bars, the walls, no in-between gone and not

freedom balanced on the final moment

on the account of the one of us who can read

walk through books, seek the chart, flatter each page

so not one letter is lazily mumbled

after dinner when the game room closes, full corridor

we peel off to each semi-private room, scuttle

across despondent brick, hiding smiles, a ray of hell

rising from the pit of our stomach aches

for all the naming of all the having

one last fighting lock of feeling

One big eye   Too big   but still vision
impaired   Is it impaired?   or supreme
dead   or transcending   dimensions

the Cyclops casts and dreams   a thrust of hero   enters
before her, calls it and backs away   knowing her self-fulfilling
Enemy, her recollection   a hero's warship, like her   a self-born storm

This island, remorseless   all variety flocks and fleeces   fattened, soft
sweetest wines, cheese   trumpet vines and hollyhocks, all species
from miniscule nubs, from nothing   with spring flowering

And her visitor comes   prodigal   the principle of sails
that air + absence = movement   fill exhaustion with motion
hungry; Tired too of air pockets   optically elusive

You're a great warrior She hails   Or Nothing
I couldn't agree more, these days I'm Nothing
And barely a wind came up to help Leaving me in irons

with Lips, of necessity   Two minimally, and perfect Segments
casting all realms into possibility   Doubt from deck   Thunder
some form of self-made Giant   Sound, my lips a Fallen horn

Unnamable, she's both and   Impossible   Beyond, an Eye, named
Cyclops, he calls out   A crisis on the welcome   She meets him there
Acrobats and beach clowns   All eyes blind and blinking

Like some great hero   I'm No One, I parry   and this treachery
good at a moment's notice   Stand behind a ship
She called "approaching"   That expanse of thought

One beach   and one horizon formed   in grotesque canvas
a monster rising in a vacant cave   Home, let me at her: Polyphemos
Replacing flocks of lambs and ewes with blood   Crafty anchor-chains

Rhetor, she asks   Born between thoughts in partial slope
Lips, how parted these stories   and a crew of men, united?
Or asunder? As if you could mourn their deaths one by one?

My fame   Face, it's said Goes up to heaven, all this world's wealth
creating an Is of me, and Isle Yours, cannot Not be   This trick
No matter how Lawless   a peak of snow-ribboned   Landscape

Restored, a one-eyed species lower-down than most
beached   Hurricane-like   delivering a visitor
with many parts   all hands   afraid of no one

Even Kassapu: resultant name   Sanskrit for saliva?
She won't say   And sorcerer?   Some wisdom sloppy with breath? Licking lips
A platter of chips tarted with vinegar   The effluvia of a corpse

This nonexistent thing   a must?   Depart, silence   welcome
on any Island, singular Nobody's home Unmoored, unanchored   Is a ship a labor?
I've got some bread on board, offerings   But there are no Gods, she whispers

Hurricane hunters   Penetrate the eye   an onset of perspective?
An island solid only by reflection?   *Ratio?*   *Oratio?*   She won't say
despite shanks of pink beads along branches; a scattered suburbia

Beaten, as I was, off my course   by winds one minute   from every direction
another minute beset by calm   Forsaking compasses   we ran headless
finding only clouds for stars   A second thought   and another followed it

What journey, city   feels like an answer   From the captain, greetings
remote swamp   questions   open in a thousand lifetimes
bobbing to shore   View of unsubstantiated groves   shrubs and grasses

Ten inches snow   at the mention   the thought reverses   A hundred suns
Cherry blossoms knit with ice   deployed by squirrels, jumping
mud and river silt   A sprawl,   nine hundred laminated bowls

How much riddle can be resolved?   Rings of birds, riding waves
One curse, one motion   Muted in opposing faces, one giant eye
Indifferent to famine, self-made   Self-thought, fed and sown

The big wind   from a warm ocean   arising from nothing? I snort
And named?   elements coiled in snakes   Grows old and dies
hundreds of miles later   some ecstatic sweep   *Hunraken*

of character, set in a path on a revolving world   Quiet for a long period after
Sea-storm untracked virgin   Five hundred million million horsepower
Alone, Cyclone   a simple wind equaling several thousand hydrogen bombs

She wonders aloud   Where I'm going?   But I'm the son of <u>so</u> and <u>so</u>
or daughter of each motion's cause   Troy and other battles
Wore me down to Nothing   a notion causing panic   a terminal statement

split across mother and father   foreign lands and home   sun upon wind upon wave
homelessness, anyway   Exile of a Hero, misfit   Nothing yearns for us, carelessly
it's we who yearn, the boat forced on   Existing, to carry phenomenal cargo

Soggy and lilting windward   masts and mainsails gone   Aha! the evidence
merely some matter receding   from Speaking   Such forms   deceived by Water
into Water, the fate of objects which senses make   Fate   offers obstructions

Solids cause ripples the Noumenon of epic legends: concept, images, Distance
Between names The men of family Seeing themselves? the Giant wonders
How does anyone think all this? She reels back her Eye unconcealing history

In praying, totally Heroes should Dwell eliminate Journeys Marvel and rest
Behold waters Offer, fall up to heaven Reflection, how much Insight
does one eye provide? he demands, devouring my soldiers without hunger

That steely ball, blue and tearing becomes a mirror sticking there, I vertigo
toward all those legendary landings, hostile incarnations of battling demons I set myself
apart in battle Questions? Some Socrates, testing the one who says he's Just, a splinter

Never to fear one action's dictum: Lips? Ecstatic circular systems, Part
and not Loudly she responds with more questions Ending this scene quickly
Dying back to the island Taking my ship and others in my own translation

Funeral? Not yet, she winks A symptom's flap a wait, for skin peeled
like birch bark blisters the desiccation of lips in a closed system Answer
what nothing opposes the Cyclops rests Gains speed and rushes into draining space

You'll see, she says   Tides=higher   waves=slower coming   lips=cunning
the distant veil of ice crystals   six veils of a finish line ripped abruptly
another Hurricane nearing   Human Condition   recycling   water=vapor

Oh spiraling broken-hearted Cyclops   hitting the coast, You'll destroy yourself
the more power swells when aroused   Fattened flocks approach her
all heart, liver, bowel   The monster picks up two of my companions, Bashes

Their heads together, and on rock   Their brains return   to darkest matter
And stop the flow, no tears   A large wave breaks, others stand   still in motion
Victims, she warns, fare better   than murderers

And all she sucks up   Corrupt   that greeting off the cliffs   No help echoes
What again, she asks   Is your name?   And this one's easy answer pales   in my previous
Miasma, driven by riddles   Nobody, without a lie   This is not a list

Of attributes, she rejects   an out-dated possibility   of returning Home, finally
one mouth born of two lips overused   Overfed, the lambs fear Night
the gates   before   A hundred children of the Sun drag the ship's carcass to shore

43

It looks like you're staying   this way   Out of the usual way   of others
sebaceous glands, smooth and hairless   swell when aroused, stiffened
Nerveless, Lips: speaking something, You came to my Island   Linked

with subjects; She cuts the corpses into entrails and meats, Devours   a waterspout
subject now of her own proposition; Wait, the entrance blocked   Exit then, no night
no day   A battle between warm and cold;   air, this paradox of discrimination

Resolving the dual limitations of climatic imagination   pure, this mind
This beach's distance from my feet   there is no beach   these are not feet
No one's eating something; Am I cannibal enough? What distance is too close?

An eye seeing itself? Oh, get on now! I think   You eyed my vessel
Whatever I gave in already: I always am that Nobody   dissolving postcards
One wind=No wind   Miasma's riddle: how one eye centers a system, unborn

Eating my own crew   my flesh   she sops the fluids up with fleece, rocks slick
with organ juices, brilliant darkness   day and night revolve before me, a ride
across the mountains   stepping out onto clouds   panicking, revolution, swooning

Arguable;   she brings up language   As though changing the subject
So what?   Wide open sounds on the breath stream: /A:/
the only One which doesn't take the air for anything Open and spontaneously arriving

As a word homes in, blocking passage   smooth as wet glass, licked
the tongue that greets   the traveler   or membranes, the mouth goblet
biting the lips, or sucking death from corpses: dirt-tinged liquids, minerals

A single drop falls   Spreads inflection   Soaks the neutral sand with colors
Appearing folded in   concealing, my army eaten   as Dawn, once called
"rosy fingered"   fucks them   nameless "one for all";   A dream Nobody came?

This stable omnivorous arrangement   Nothing eternal   Nothing doing
Nobody moving   Or who's using all these monemes   To con the dreamers
"the stable hearts" of "well-enclosing unconcealment"   Oblivion

On the distance   A veil of ice crystals   and a bar of low clouds
one night can't be found   weather's not mortal the way I intend it   this path
following   something you feel? I ask   No Wind?   Or a hurricane? she asks

Does one eye take it all in,   Constructively, wisest unwisely asking
what won't she say? miasma or hurricane: both "sloppy with breath"
Lips scabbed off in hardened peels Taking half the morning nod, chirping birds

Getting a real grip on this chapter, I was half in the land of Miasma, just returned
from over-interpreting Oracles Can't it wait? I wondered This trip one enormous
lack of entrails More sleep Here's her unreasonable eye lid

Blind! I call knowing blindness at least, she warns is better
than your measly apparatus: Unborn? Undying — neither one goodbye nor many
Born from what? Self? I ask Lips tipped back apart, ecstatic Nobody can help

"And so she greeted me at that place" Are you one, she asked or just old epic
and who are these remaindered? A knot of vomiting sailors; We're headed up home
the Goddess laughed Conceived as a category? Oh, not so much that as one

Opposed to another a Finite journey or what? I've got none of that,
this path dangerous and overgrown is and isn't absolute across the horizon, which appears
As it disappears, all like minded ships she and I, sworn of the same silence

46

how she must think I cling to scene   my One-and-Only   colorless
for instance: green   beyond which, she continues   nobody comes, causing confusion
hurricane season   in an ocean heating and air cooling   and what isn't can soon kill

She puts on a coat and boots   Made first from books, Attributed
A whole wardrobe, empty of a closet   Or just the sting of contradictory moods
You'll choose, perhaps to stay   Perhaps leave, but deceit and Heroics

Meet me in Speech, with What she says, what she Doesn't Say
Contemplating   a surface   Inner, she sets it back   *Panta rhei*, Not again! aching
I laugh — goddess this lingerie   tempting castaways! You're no match, I shout

Encrusted with holes: oh, bully!   There is no such hole in the sky, she scolds
a shadow of a cloud   covering this meeting with pause   Days=balloons
sent in to measure   the Pressures   barometers   radar reflectors

And so could I harness invisibility before this mirror   If I unthought this
sneak up   disguised in the Abundant   leaves rustling
A good trick   see me, inseparable from land or sea or sheep   it's my nerves

Cold air sinks, heavy   Sometimes slipping, rolls over   The warm air, a tongue
sucks down this raging vacuum   two-eyes battle: here and not
bringing down other autonomies   corresponding identities   everybody talks

about the weather, but nobody does   anything   suddenly, and nothing
happens until a movable organ   Capable of discussion, like Why did we come?
To this or any land, Itself an obstacle to wind: /p/   /b/   /m/   /w/

A dialogue for a martyr   originally   Now a beach of 100 Socrates   lips
and a few unexpurgated Buddhas   bathing   not from Ideas, but a dumb show   parted
caught in a train   before commuting, a layer of junkyards   Death stalled dying

A fatty patch, hoods open   dried-out tongues rotting   rusted open
car-casses, stripped   Is Nothing visible?   Cities everywhere?   And Cyclones
heave the clouds on loaded backs   A year's worth of rain in a single minute

One parsed moneme: an eruption   Visible speech
A tongue runs over and is cut; her one-eye jumps   The salve a Knife   Naming
All she has the heart to say   *Baguois*?   the signless cloud

48

Too justified for parentheses; uncountable syllables gaining force   and then one night . . .
concealed by appearances . . .   She follows my gaze back to itself   all Twisting
Papagallos   and No One's name, a denominator apparently spiraling, Vowels

then don't designate segments, she towers about me: What's this air's motion?
Where does it come from? Where does it go?   Where is it found?
What is stillness?   Another thought of death or home?   Washing up, Can you find it?

trovados   visible systems   Wayfaring   arbitrary clouds
this mind undone, it's in my throat   my heart   my skin   these bleeding
wounds, my dying broken-bodied men   all this in my heart, despite the twist

Put forth of the babble of a rotating earth: the storms move north   and clockwise
since clocks are wise   again obscured   but then one night . . .   the wind dies down
concealed in what it looks like, divided noun from noun   hot from cold

becoming dangerous, waves gaining height   blurred, a hard attack:
I call this "bad" — but "b" is not the choice   is it "sad"?   that "b"
one simple moneme is not, in a closed inventory   this necessity

How no one acts or speaks   and shatters   mutely, a hero taking his sword
rather than demonstrate cowardice   in one   society, or one closed-in
family, lonely choice proscribed,   to say what's "sad" at the moment of "bad"

mysteriously from a storm of no wind;   the miasma of an unborn undying hurricane
Veering east, a boat pushed out   cannot exist   but suck the outside off   a pocket
an immediate collapse   on principle   there is no feeling

A slightly pouting set of isobars   where flesh parts ways   the Eye watching itself
at the lowest point of pressure   Storm's Center   inventories hollering
willy-willies   A million names   *ta feng*   this ancient word spun out

What can you really see? I provoke her with a stick   Signal my crew to forge a splinter
You are some Aim, I taunt   No, you are, she returns   If you say something, you add
And then you aren't   Laughing, my men send up a cheer   To even say One, we adduce

Is to speak false   As you describe yourself   No One   called so, before a mother
Possessing nothing   supremely dependent, sure   of every being   unalloyed
Remote from all contingency   This Island paradise   unassociated   Who can map it?

But, not   Interrupting, she asks   That One you speak   does not apply
but to some-one in relation, and that, from my point of view   is impossible
So my cause does not do, but is done   To me, storms and calm   fair both good

Your two eyes master the perceptions of depth, death   frightening you to appear
necessarily you self-appear to many, a hero's welcome   they follow   fallow, fallible
But, unsaying this itself is Said   Notice the plenty of rain and sun, all that grows

All your hungers yearn for This, all thirst   All lives suffer from thoughts which kill
in a moment remorselessly   Beyond which you'll never know   Renounce it, and stay
produce every man off your ships   For blood and meat   And Stay, enthusiastic

Stably spoken incinerates character   a beach fragment   a monstrous idea
hangs a body down them like a towel from a peg   an eye blind to its own pupil
author of my ship   Licks lips the softest membrane   bloody

set of qualities, How many are you? she asks   Nobody at all, I lie   in debt
hiding all the *praxis* in honeyed *lexis*, pitting appearance   against all ships
tucked in the bay behind the bluff   if we do not heed the warning, it will kill us

I plot: One-eye   Cannot distinguish sand from flesh, or Me
from my crew, the dogs, rats   the gulls overhead   all flush in one supreme present
and filling to the borders   there's only being, handicapped   She stumbles depthless

Becoming what she won't say I think   she would argue   epochs split in seconds
Non-appearing reasons to believe Nothing Or   some mortality beyond any count
Why she's compelled finally to see no one coming   and cast a hero to slay her

to unfold stocky goats and escape   Judging for herself, she stays mortal for a moment
With me and the ship, some high political action   Dialectic half-human, concealed
as present   laid upon the landing   Trumped up   and still reasoning   I wake?

This vision cannot stay as it began   The wind, inferior to its source, the light
pale apricot light   misty greenish light   purple rose of light   colors doubling, change
You conceive this as impossible   How so? As though deep and drunk

Air splits   Across the weather   Watery evaporating process   To this *doxa* land
only solid for a moment   Nothing escapes here   not   Trick questions
How can you remain so empty, I taunt Oh, dreaming, she asks: Dawn?

Do you think one day you'll sail alone   Leaving this one eye land

meaningless as whatever was   Oblivion   Everything green

Or eaten?   Or called?   at Once   Colorless of every hue

Her eye bulging open, inviting   willfully   Wide as a wheel, ribboned with vessels

bleeding, smeared from duct to lash   I step up   A shadow passes in that enormous retina

Deeply she perceives no one   and my mortal vision, split in two   frames a legend

As long as the giant wind stays at sea   hiding heat in the building storm

picking up water   fueling   violence, mute   It Lives

a pair of lips, as equal crushing reason   paralipsis: I'm not even saying this

Rhetor, she calls and I look away   public speaker   on inefficient tongue

what Nobody dares say, you speak   poorly, unconvincingly   the fleshy spoon

what lips do nothing, are those lips? She taunts   and I run a look   on the single

horizon, a dialogue lasting a million days   Then one night   unobstructed final

inaudible, remembered   beyond the waves   nobody's force, or by wind

shapely modifying air   a cavity, full   you'll never improve

This inexperienced presentation   one is the same as ten, except when you're weak
deluded, softened by grief   some sport, this massacre
unless someone wiser, a tutor   teaching modulations of speed, pauses for emphasis

Skillful in thinking beyond low and high   and named across the audience
the world revolving   Believe me, she continues   you suck at this stuff, I know
my Aim's gone, I can't live by word of mouth   work for an hour on every sentence

practice every phrase   for meaning, emphasis   the point is to communicate
the weight   What proof except the smashing of rocks on ships   how do I witness you
or gravity? You pull appearing effects, traces of what once moved

Her eye overflows itself   And loses no fluid   Trickery? I fall, stunned
Your fullness is unfounded   hunts cause in some effect   your seeing
Me, you see   No one, remember   terrible heat-trapper, the sun a powerful motor

Lament, then   Polyphemos   my companions misunderstand   how you suck up water
Nobody calls and nobody answers hurricane season Her one-eye open in wonder
no wonder! wild-eye in the purple-rim   to no one, then, I'll offer absolute gifts, she warns

Ink on paper = pen, lead me   to a meal   strictly for returning heroes
saliva changes with one's passions and no one sees   How you really feel
a saliva-drinker can with one taste tell   if you've been dreaming

All manner of destruction resulting   Electric systems out   Battleships   snapped
and beachfronts   sewers backing up   flipping the surface under   tree roots
breached   The captain's breath, just a trap door ripped off   a church

in which a vacuum forms, low pressure   creating the evacuation of air
What you won't tell me   stories make bodies   pulling the beings
out of existence, walls explode, down   Barns, bricks   becoming Bullets, nails

fly to uncovered faces   Oncoming wires, signs
veils of splinters, hot spears charred in the wind, fires start spontaneously
send children flying, one hundred pounds per inch, and all this

Just a warning that worse   Self-born from nobody out in the center   Wind
an ocean's womb, a scrap of paper   Empty   bag   this solid house, Cyclops
full force against a tree   five to eight tons   send it through concrete

55

But even this unbirthing,   undying   must return   clockwise, or landing
make contact destroy and learn this hand this face, the tempting foods
fruits of rain   which is not apart, of clouds   lending nonsense

This simple stick becomes a Spear   this Eye its resting place   a Madness
all hell pulling up your anchors, like weeds the markers picked, like flowers
collected, your two eyes deceive Sick with wishing calmer waters

I thrust deeply in her gelatinous sphere   Cleaving into Two that globe
which watches even as it spurts   albumen-like,   froth and blood
in actual progress of an Idea   sputters another Riddle   worded in its limit

Where earthquakes follow   Typhoon's twin   Where one split splits another
Engenders tsunami   cyclone=*Hunraken's* strain on the sea bed
and in all these collisions   even ill wind blows nobody good, she rages

From the unceasing heating of water pumping between two chambers
all the differentiated cells   the birth place   hurricanes
always moving north   pulsing, rotating like a wheel

56

One is not, without   I kneel, therefore   impossibly, You are not
and I, cannot not be   thus violence is useless   Thirsty for my crew's blood
the legends tell   All this dialogue and warning, pursuing the blind

with signless clouds   Your eye, even   I tell her, stays impossible
despite this place, knowing islands arise   from many points
coordinate this one position   I'll spare your beach, horizon

And you'll have Nobody to Thank   and yourself for the Pain of losing sight
And all hands on deck are one when this story ends   or at my return
"This Nobody, who I think has not yet got clear of destruction," her throat rasps

Becalmed in what's empty   the burden   This Nobody gave me
and you, I retort   What's one thing gotten you?
A twisting power, centered nowhere but the outrageous dream of sky

Lament, Polyphemos   setting out, I'll forget This Ecstasy   atoll
the low bar of clouds   my crew and ship, The reflection of a teary   wavering
certain Eye, bereft   cut straight through with nobody's spear splintered

today and tomorrow   Oblivious we sail   stuffed with oracles
Stepping right into spiraling   Recording smells and senses, riddles
this violent episode   stops or doesn't   Land or not

her split temperature brings the surface turmoil to battle some giants
a planet spinning a storm   uninhabitable, this one
I remind her, Used to be so brutally liveable

Against the trial of pre-told tales   called to any mouth
My lips stay closed when yours say, "No one by cunning kills me, and not by force"
Home or nowhere   a Hero,   two eyes   open two eyes   shut

a gap the space of an ocean
gap, cleft, break, rift or hole
an event traveled by electric spark — a spark gap
an opening in a mountain range — unpassable otherwise
a suspension of continuity — for the sake of right timing
an absence of information — used to distinguish segments
in a recording medium — gaping light at the partition of a wall
cleft like a door ajar — easily pushed by wind
or the distance between the head of a recording device
and the surface of the medium — fillable with sound

no — you say — but yes

the sound of the space of an entire ocean of space

Alaska: that toward which the action of the sea is directed.

    Flag: Eight gold stars in a field of blue (seven in *Ursa Major*, the eighth the
        North Star, *Polaris*)

    Motto: North to the future.

    Flower: Forget-me-not.

    East-West travel is the history of the highway.

    North-South the steamboats.

    Up-Down, railroads.

June 7, 1942: Japanese forces land by sea on the Aleutian islands of Attu
    and Kiska.

May 11, 1943: U.S. forces land on Attu, retaking it after 18 days, the only
    battle fought on "U.S. soil" in WWII. Kiska is evacuated secretly
    by the Japanese on July 23. We might name a baby 'Kiska' after
    capture and escape. We might name a baby 'home' after the flavor
    of territory.

Juneau: 90 miles NE of Sitka; 580 miles SE of Anchorage; 980 miles NW
    of Seattle. Theistic: A place of dreams. A Panhandle. Seismic Zone
    2. Glaciers in Southeast Alaska mostly recede, except the Taku.
    Nevermind the age when we became intoxicated, wondrous, and
    were moved. Echo Cove marks the end of the existing Juneau road
    system to the north. The age when prospects ran straight to the
    blood. We might name a baby "Taku" for advancing; "Echo" pride
    in vain, or "Seismic," "Wonder." Taku River runs south from the
    end of the existing road in Thane.

1960's: eight major surveys tested the viability of getting roads in or out of
    Juneau. From anywhere anywhere. Tests are still done today, with
    engineers and surveyors conjuring words for land connection:

artery, umbilical. There is something to driving in and out by tunnels, bridges. Something terrible about rising into open air, something about the direction of the action of the sea. Juneau tidal currents can be four or six knots because of fjords 200-300 feet deep at the shoreline. Tides average 15-feet. Bears die on the roads getting to the water; perhaps we protect the name "Bear" for the crossing.

Too bad: so many reasons. Now we think we are realistic. The rising feeling. Where we're headed. An incessant question. Maiden in a warrior's voyage, prostrate to every inception. Apply certain uncertainty to the reflected horizon. To what we want, we can't know before. We dream we are a family. A turning foundation. The action of the sea. The direction of the past: a modest heroic. What if the inscrutable womb was salt or fog or repeats this purification: miscarriage. With such a thing, we might call the baby "Bomb" or "Travel Plan."

First fatal bird strike: 1912. A gull jammed in the controls of a plane. Birds clog air intake screens on the turbo engines, causing insufficient thrust and the plane stalls, crashes. Multiple bird strikes occur when you mess up a flock. For jet engines and turbine engines birds collide with windshields, landing gear, leading edges of wings, stabilizers, fuselage. At the christening we could mumble "Windshield" or "Gull."

1929: the first flight makes it from Alaska to San Francisco in one day. 1935: First amphibious plane augments the railway service, flying-boat engine-moths between layered wings. After WWI: bush planes the only way to leave the sea and find oneself inland. Lives saved; made. Deliveries. Yukon Southern Air Route run by the Yukon Seldom landed on water, rivers or lakes, ice in winter. Land of marsh-flower mothers sweet to the seeds. 1940: first commercial air service lands in Juneau on a gravel airstrip in the

pasture of a dairy farm. Lodestars "hop" from Juneau to Seattle in
seven hours. But in wartime '41, the 'Northwest Staging Route'
spreads bases for light aircraft from Great Falls, Montana to far-off
Fairbanks. Built to supply and shore up defense in the new born
war. Might we name a baby after its own collateral: "Tissue,"
"Montana."

History: a plan for engineering across unplanned passages. What might
have dropped to the deepest part of the information became
instead a shallow skim. Layered on like clothes and muscle, the
news of light. And nowhere to tell this news but the frequent
approach to the question and organizing some quicker baggage. At
the point of lineage we get helped across the important ocean; the
docking areas farther from the birthing ones. Might the name be
"Skim" for how we fear and repeat this; "Runway" or "Jet" for the
time of winging it. Any marriage might advance the news of
movement, progress. Or alternatively, just love into it. Not toward.
Not moving but for the guarantee of waves either way.

Juneau airport: 9 miles northwest of downtown. The airport covers 640.55
acres of land. Directly south and east of the airport is a wildlife
refuge. There is one east-west paved runway (8456 feet long by
150 wide, along magnetic alignment of 80/260 degrees and 26 feet
above sea level). Runway 26 is served by a blast pad and parallel
taxiway (75 feet wide and runs from the approach end of Runway 8
east, ending short of the approach end of Runway 26). The lack of
full parallel taxiway means that 737 and 727 aircraft had to use the
east portion of the runway for taxi purposes when landing on 8 or
departing on 26, causing delays. The narrowness of the channel
precluded any approach or departure to the southeast. The aircraft
had to fly visually from an approach point on Coghlan Island,
3.2 nautical miles from the airport. No go-around could be
commenced from this point because of the mountains. Meanwhile,
we consider names like "Square Feet" and "North." Family names.

Traveling causes the central sensation in the order of possible triumph. Not to mention the ways we could imagine holding an idea accelerating into daylight. From learning, we might "Approach" the name, or "Baby" even, "Circling." Three runway exits connect runway to taxiway. A blame-balance triumphs in this whirl, and yet mightn't we say "Taxiway" or "Refuge" despite "Runway," or "Delay."

A proposal: extend the taxiway eastward along runway 8/26 for 3700 feet. This meant culverting 300 feet of lower Jordan Creek, filling 25 acres of wetland and filling or draining a 7.25 acre pond. Construction would have to allow critical fish passage: meaning no construction between April 1 and May 31 and Sept 1 and Oct 31. The upstream reaches of Jordan Creek are the most populated salmon stream for juveniles in the Juneau area. Salmon use the pond for resting and ripening, staying 10-15 days before pounding upstream to shallow spawning water. The proposal included additional culverted passage under the taxiway that the migrating salmon would negotiate to get to upper Jordan Creek. Pools, channel construction, limited meanders, grade increases and cover would be designed to offer alternatives to the fish. Check-dams made from logs or rocks could create deeper runs and scour pools. We could name the baby "Parent" or "Anadromous" for rerunning; "Parent" or "Semelparous" for dying after the first spawning.

Once inside the Terminal: 22,000 square feet. Expansion to north and south are constrained, eastward by the new parking lot and westward by the apron area of the runway. Lines of people cross every inch moving like this love letter between mile-posts. They've crossed the lower waters already. "Landing" we might call the baby, for all that's rushing up; a rising, "Terminal." We predict happiness and misery. Nothing new under sun or storm. A continued home for houses of trial: theater. Worship. A continued basket for orphans. We predict a continually sullied enlightenment

until all arrivals and the flame-pure fuel dissolves the tunnels back
into the departure. Home? Perhaps we will be no more lucky than
this. X-rays scan the luggage for skeletons, knives, washing
implements, harvest tools, baby mammals; fruits of labors, harvest.
Worse the abduction of beauty by the brine of emotions, or that
which washes out the sharp brilliant flow to the cortex and
hemispheres of the brain. Desire makes the impulses soggy. The
arrival is heavy and numb. At the terminal the stuffed bodies of land
creatures stand fixed in "Black Bear." "Polar." A glass of chemical
corpses beyond their shelf lives. "Raptor" and "Shorebird"
dioramas.

A recent crash: an Alaska Airlines 737 and a salmon dropped by an eagle.
The fish hit the window at the top of the cockpit causing no
serious damage. Consequently, the airport applied to fill and
dredge ponds to make them unattractive to "bird hazards." The
tension between what love creates, creativity itself our chore, our
form, and the outward look of wanting to tangibly repeat
ourselves, hold an ongoing stare. Together we spread bodies
onstage, but opening ours?

By sea: after the Russian purchase in 1867, regular boat service starts
between U.S. ports and Sitka for the dispatch of occupation
troops. Of course the locals already crossed water, along with
whalers, sealers, traders in other histories navigated by canoe and
kayak. Some say that story, untrammeled, forecloses this. Still
Juneau got called Fliptown, a thriving place after an 1881 gold
strike at Treadwell. Ambitious building in brush, muskegs, and
devil's club, all in a period of competition between coast towns and
their sea-vessels: the Al-ki overtaking the Willapa even after the
Willapa had a five hours' headstart from Juneau. Or the Topeka
narrowly beating the Willapa to Wrangell, only to get overtaken
by the Willapa on the next leg. During the Gold Rush even the
most unseaworthy vessels got launched over sunken mountains.

Soon the routes bypassed Juneau for Dyea; no wharfs, and horses just dropped into the sea. Fog walls, ice bergs, reefs of cutting rock, enormous tide-swept channels. No radios, no helpful maps. All charts hungry for light. Renewable rush of individual secretion, an info-matic system. "Secret" after what we would be forced to protect and keep. "Al-ki" or "Coast" for the slap of water. "Tlingit" spelled and respelled. "Fog." There was no radar, sonar; instead to make it down the narrow channels, captains blew whistles and listened to the echoes to be sure they were in the deepest middle. The charts themselves were covered with P.D.s (*Position Doubtful*) and E.D.s (*Existence Doubtful*) and dotted areas *Unsurveyed*. If you were losing time and distance (measured by speed and channel lights) you ended like a salmon "smelling your way" on your own best bet.

Land (a lock): A prison and a haven. (Water) we can't manage to own; waiting for luck in the Age of Ownership. Waiting for them to get us over. We allow an infant a stranger allowance, homed into our uncertain opening of story swelling and receding at the edges. We might name the baby "History" for the welcoming of strangers to this house.

The gold-rush stampeders' journey: boat to Dyea, hike Chilkoot trail 30 miles to Lake Bennett, build a boat and float 500 miles down Yukon to Dawson City and the gold fields. Steepest terrain was called the Golden Stairs. Any beast who could pull or carry or drag or haul anything more than itself was taken, and often discarded unfed, unwatered, in the gulch. Oxen, mules, dogs, horses perished in this place. If nothing crossed over from this world into "the next" we wouldn't believe anything about death except the relatively rapid decay of the body and its movements. What we imagine is the solid frontier of our world. The airplane a public agreement, a managed communion, what was originally someone's daydream put together in the public trust bolt by bolt so that we all believe it. Skyscrapers, cars, the stock exchange: artifacts of ideas which have come true. Invention doesn't arise in the science, within the laws and properties of matter. Not until imagination hardens into consensus does the shape of putting a boat in the water use existing grammar to shape a further act. Boat. Plane. We walk by and take it in. That man's dream slips easily to ours. Thus the name "Baby" or "Roof" then, or "City."

Railways: standard gauge is 4'8-1/2", narrow is 3'; White Pass route out of Skagway. No prospector wanted to work for wages with all the gold just waiting in the Klondike. Who would stay and build the railroad? Most were stuck in Skagway for one or another reason and wage-worked long enough to get to the gold fields or back home. 700-2000 workers a day, though a rumor of a gold strike would clear the railbeds in a second. Bed had to be blasted out of solid rock. 21 miles to the summit, sea level to 2885 feet. A 250 ft tunnel was hand dug through solid granite, the only tunnel on the 110-mile rail trail. Steel cantilever bridge built across Dead Horse gulch below the summit arched 215 feet. A switchback was used to get around the gulch until this was completed. Railwork paid 3 dollars for 10 hr day, not including meals. 40 miles from Skagway to Lake Bennett. The next 27 miles lay along the lake to Carcross and then to Whitehorse. But by the time north and south rails met, the gold rush had moved to Nome, and barely a pocketful of men stood there as the last spike went through. If no one comes, will we laugh when we call it "Empty" or "Barren"?

World War, 1940-42: military Alaska. Gold, copper, whalebone, canned salmon, fur — all these were over. Only war was left to liven up the wilderness economy. Alaska Steam taken over by the War Shipping Administration, painted the ships grey. Zigzag courses set under submarine alert. June 3, Dutch Harbor bombed. No lights onboard after dark. Guns up forward, windows boarded. After the war, boats all wrecked or sold off, and very few ships continued along the Inside Passage, eliminating stops at Haines and Skagway.

Then in the early 50's, a series of strikes (sailor's union, marine cooks and stewards' union) cost the steam company over half the vessels still sailing. Costs got awful: moving supplies to 200,000 people spread over 580,000 square miles of territory up and down a ragged coast. Army DC-4s (4-engines) and the army airfields all became available after the war: Annette Island, Cordova, Anchorage, Fairbanks, King Salmon. Air service essentially stomped out the steamers by '54 and only a few cargo carriers ran until the 1970's tourist boats and cruise ships flooded in. With the resurgence of mining and oil, the Alaska Marine Highway System year-round service finally linked Bellingham, WA to Haines via Juneau, where the new Auke Bay terminal opened 11 miles north of downtown. We might name the baby "Passenger" or "Zigzag" in the nest of number-kin, docked right at the risk or "Adventure" for a premature birth; a kind violence muted in words. "Bay," a rugged formula: a baby dreams without knowing the word for it, or "June" for lupine along the highway. "July" called fireweed, flower of the north. Biggest dandelions you've ever seen.

On land: the "Al-Can" highway from Dawson to Fairbanks, conceived to connect air bases as fast as possible to avoid the Japanese invasion of Alaska. Connection of air by land, against the sea. Make the new state secure through the advertisement of another identity. The U.S. army took over the lease and operation of the railway during the war years: 770th Railway Operating Battalion of the Military Railway Service, Oct, 1942. Engines 10 and 14 shipped north from Tennessee, nos 20 and 21 from Colorado, nos 22, 23, 24 from Silverton Northern. In 1943, 10 steam engines consigned to Iran were diverted to Skagway and converted from metered gauge to narrow. The total accumulated: 36 engines and 300 freight cars. All engines 2-8-2s built by Baldwin, and all scrapped or sold after the war. 1959: Alaska renamed the 49th U.S. State.

On land: the Alaska Highway connected to Edmonton only because of Pearl Harbor. Decided by a Special Cabinet Committee, the route was incidental to getting something built. Roosevelt's signature on the project four days from Committee to decision. Time or the Japanese closing behind them, biological survival clock countdown spurring them on. The pioneer tote road supplying the troops would be the first phase. The Public Roads Administration would handle the affair, with the help of army engineers. Where no maps were available they'd just play the road by ear, artists of uncertainty, often led by dogs. 35th Combat Engineer Regiment moved by rail to Edmonton and then to Dawson Creek. Then a winter march over a trail 300 miles northwest to Fort Nelson. After the thaw and runoff they began cutting tote road toward Contact Creek 219 miles west, greeting the soldiers from the 340th Regiment who had punched through south from Whitehorse. The 18th Combat Regiment went to Skagway. The road had to be passable by October. Someone went on snowshoes, looked in the right direction, hacked the trees, blazed them, and bulldozers followed behind. The first maps were bad. Rivers were out of place or left off. Not accurate enough to build a road. Muskegs, lakes and mountains weren't marked at all. This was the Pioneer Survey. Then came aerial mapping with cameras. The road was put down in seven months. "Corduroy" the swamp by laying logs and brush across. Ended up totally crooked. Arctic clothes and rations that would withstand freezing were sent from G-4, supply. The Haines Road over-mountain went to the sea while the other road went a winding 1400 miles to Fairbanks. A stream bursts from nowhere, but then we notice two ovaries of snow on either side at a certain height. Glaciers give of themselves. Some take back. As the time approaches, we start to think of names like "Spruce" or "Winter" for the atmosphere; "Soldier" or "Corps" to register the harm. Bottomless muskegs: pits or bogs of rotten organic muck overgrown with reindeer moss, small spruce, and tamarack. Sinkholes: large land floating on deep water, the moving floor of the boreal forest. Bog blueberries cover them. Frozen at night. Range of mountains never crossed by foot. Feet are a cultural

measure we like to think; Poetry. Like what hasn't been here.
American soldiers rode rumbling C8 Cat bulldozers through
tangles of taiga. They made the Al-Can/Alaska Highway crooked so
if the enemy did ever land they couldn't follow it. Smart-ass rookie
engineers. No drainage, dodging potholes and creeks. Modeling the
road on the river which used to be the best means of travel.
"Muskeg"; "Sand." Opening ceremony of the Pioneer Highway
took place at Kluane Lake, Nov. 20, 1942.

November 1942: orders came for the Haines road between the Al-Can and
Haines, finally to the sea. Civilians under PRA finished much of
that project by Dec 31, 1943. Cost 13 mil. Bridges were going out
ten or fifteen a day. Mud Hill. Couldn't keep the ground in place.
Covered in tons of stone, drove piles sixty feet long and tied them
together to hold up road, all ended in valley. By 1943, the
Japanese war was focusing solely on the South Pacific and leaving
the North alone. Changed the highway plans and most equipment
was left abandoned, or burned. Can we name a child "Alaska" for
the action which is directed toward the sea?

Time and location: stars and the angle of the horizon reveal where we must
be standing. Clouds overhead and underfoot. Fog rising from the
forests and the timeless disorientation of time when there is no
light to read the clock, and waking up in the dark winter hours to
hear the hope of light, eagles chirp or call for miles. A first alarm
clock fills the rivers with water which fills the lakes which rise and
set the docks in motion, tilting the cars so they run downhill
bumping into a runway which starts a crank which flips a switch
and pops the plug from the balloon which lifts off and floats
westward pulling the rope which trips the airplane which takes off
in the sky which leaves a wake of air which pushes the clouds and
causes the lightning which hits the flag pole which leads to the
ground which shakes the table and tips the candle which burns the
house and fills the room with smoke and sets off the smoke alarm

and wakes you up to stop the flames and stay awake to the future as always for the little things.

The male spawning sockeye: hooked jaw and humped back. Green face and splotchy brown eye, with dear intelligence gleaning on the look and chin. Some dappled forehead, ragged teeth, a downward smile close-up peering roundishly into a curved lens. Curved world. The red shoulders and back, a helpless beacon of color. The salmon need to rest, gathering in familiar pools, quiet hidey-holes before ascending the steepest part of the river. Transformed by the freshwater of their birth back into humped, hulking aggressive spawners. Millions of fish are carried by barge around dams, fake lakes, concrete, sleek rivers, etc. Ground up by turbines. To save them you have to put boulders in the rivers, put bends back, create pools. Rills reconnecting to mainstreams. Culvert laddered. Repair graveled-over streams that made roads, driveways. Streams downcut when they've lost structures dissipate their ability to pool and gather resting places. Catching our shadows, the fish dart away. But in the dusk they can't see the shadows and so might be called simply "Coho" or "King."

In a stream: fight against the current, don't let go. Rest. Don't backslip or get pushed along the shore. Use a rock or fallen branch to wait behind. Fins like broken bird wings flop in small ripples. All that is visible of the Chinook. Wearing special spawning colors: silver, smokey-reds. Wild males. Smelling the last ice age, the hands of the fishermen, the nickly bottoms of boats. Beside us the pale, scaleless fleshy pink wonders, nose down ancestors just past before. We're always one last leap away from that, but we know what's coming at least, *after*. Headwater born. Head births. Reds. Beds in the watershed. Rotting in shreds, salmon nutrients from the sea get spread through the stomachs of bear, otter and eagle and into the coniferous forests. Great crowds, creatures of all kinds, welcome the exhausted runner. The corpses rot quickly into the stream,

dissolving to feed their own babies on their first trip out. Changing
quickly from alevins to fry (fingerlings) to smolt, the babies head
tail-first toward the ocean, backing through the mirror into the
future so they'll know what it looks like when they see it head-on.
Navigating backward out to sea, they eat their parents' flesh, the
giant, knife-toothed, blade fisted, humpbacked muscle-monsters
that grew and grew from and into them.

The efforts: continue passionately. Quaint thinking of corners and stuffy
space; surprised to find it's nothing more than our poem and yet its
flaw that we measure it so far outward. We want Alaska because we
cherish the direction of the action. Three viable alternatives make
Juneau accessible by road from outside. On the maps the contour
interval is 100 feet. On the timeline, parents take their chance on
names, considering progeny as empty as the days' sun on the
boundless and pacific ocean. We might, we admit, name a baby
"Route" or "Road" for all that craving wheels turn against the sea.
Still, the first option is the *East Lynn Canal Route*: 85 kilometers
(53 miles) of new highway northward from Echo Cove along the
western edge of the Kakuhan Range and either cross the Chilkoot
Inlet to Haines or go along to Skagway. A primary route to Haines
would need to avoid 15 avalanche areas, five rock slide slopes,
steep drainages which are also avalanche chutes. Need 25 to 30
bridges including two major river crossings, 6 to 10 1-mile tunnels,
and many long rock cuts. Avalanche chutes require a combination
of bridges and snow sheds or tunnels. Granite and gneiss removed
from tunnels could be used as road embankment fill, riprap, or
crushed for concrete. Total miles to Seattle: 1940.

The second option: the *West Lynn Canal Route*, 65 kilometers (40 miles) of
new highway; cross Lynn Canal by ferry from Echo Cove to
William Henry Bay and follow coastline north along eastern toe of
the Chilkat Range and across Chilkat River to Haines by bridge or
ferry. This route accommodates 10-15 avalanche areas, no major

landslides, and numerous stream channel crossings. Two ferry landings and a minimum of 22 bridges, no tunnels, many high rock cuts and a lot of snow shed structures. Again, an abundance of rock fill for road construction. Avalanches are again greatest threat along this route. Total miles to Seattle: 1935.

Third: the *Taku River Route*, 195 kilometers (121 miles) of new highway from south of Juneau over the Taku Inlet/River and over the Taku Plateau to Atlin, B.C. This route would have to accommodate or avoid about 20-25 avalanche areas, numerous talus slopes. Need for up to 100 bridges, including 8 at major river crossings and up to four tunnels totaling over 3 miles. Total miles to Seattle: 1875.

Avalanches: born from loose, cohesionless snows which widen in their descent, grabbing additional unconsolidated snow. Slab avalanches are born when one cohesive layer separates from underlying layers across a broad area, detaching at all slab boundaries simultaneously. These fall faster, harder and wider, traveling 45 to 150 miles per hour. Avalanches in Juneau show recurrences every 1-5 years.

1610: Galileo Galilei discovered mountains and craters on the moon. The moon at its elliptical path's perigee: 356,400 km. Apogee: 406,700 km. Sunlight reflects from Moon to Earth in 1.3 seconds, lighting up the aspiration, the moon shining only by sunlight. A precise description of the moon's motion is one of the most difficult tasks of theoretical astronomy. Orbital velocity: 1km/sec or 3681 km/hr. Distance of moon from its earth is a mere thirty earth diameters and this is why the moon exerts its drastic yanking. The earth-moon system is in effect a double planet, orbiting around common ambivalence. The boundary between day and night on the moon is named the 'terminator'; "New Moon" for the illusion of birth; "Orbit" between thoughts of going there.

October 1959: Soviet probe Luna 3 reaches the moon and photographs the
    far side. July 1964: Ranger 7 photographs reveal pits and boulders.
    January 1966: Luna 9 sends back photos of tiny surface things.
    1969: first moon landing. The landings help survey the ground,
    make better maps for future landings. Dockings. Selenography is
    the geography of the moon. For landing purposes and flights
    scientists make maps represent moon craters as circular rather than
    elliptical (as seen from earth). Maps of the moon since the17th
    century always showed the near side, always as it appears to face
    us. Heights of moon-mountains were calculated by the lengths of
    their shadows; "Landmass" or "Adventure" for all that is taken and
    returns with renewed force. Lunar soil of regolith: incoherent
    mixture of sticky dust, small rock fragments and stones. This is the
    best material to imagine your planets solid. This shallow layer is
    on the moon's crust, 60 km deep. Below the lunar mantle 1000 km
    deep, a core with temperatures of 1300 degrees Celsius. Moon's
    magnetic field is overtly weak and there is only slight seismic
    activity, moonquakes only 1 or 2 on Richter scale. Travelers will
    find no water, not even in the rocks. And we know now that the
    moon has no atmosphere. No micro-organisms or any traces of
    any. No weather.

December 1972: Apollo manned program ends with Apollo 17, though
    three more probes of the Soviet Luna series bring back a few rock
    samples. New projects for future flights are still being planned,
    among them the installation of selenophysical moon stations,
    military bases. Surveillance maps help confuse us at home, gearing
    us up. The direction of the action of the sea. Roadless, yet might
    we name the baby "Space Flight" or "Someday" for how much we
    love this idea.

if the universe biases in favor of matter
                     collides with asymmetric results indicating
after the collision of antimatter with the rest
                     how empty space illuminates
things prevailing before falling apart
                                  (she's drowned)
                               as if there's no river

all this west-moving body
                     concealed by reflection
a face leaning over in childhood, the moon
                     under the stream a moment
a mobile above the crib, a lunatic hovering

years later aging over the bed
                     slipping in and out of consciousness
fat as a silhouette, a solipsism
                     even when human steps broadcast
from his surface, a flag into every home, normal

life resuming after a long run-out
                     yet we haven't really reached him
decades pass and we collide
                     with the punch of loneliness

our hollow encasements dulling
                     in the invitation
to connect and we waste the time
                     evolution spent gazing
up the selfish ceiling

the bottom of caged-in oceans reflect
                              the force of his mute attention
an organ of sympathy finds its use
                              what else is a moon but a response
to experience, a request for a face

an advertisement for expression
                              for gestures no one gets, slowly, yet
species chose faces and mock
                              from protozoa to whale, the nightly sitter
mouths gape at the sight, disbelief

rolled in the physiognomy of cells
                              curling through generations up to his mirror
unsafely and without much success

                     when I say what the matter is
                     what I mean rather
                                        (I hate drowning)
                                        my new thought

                     how did I get it
                                        how do I feel about it?
I want everyone to see it
                     I want no one to see it
                                        it's all mine
I don't really know it
                     I fear it's not right
                                        it won't last
I'm falling for a lie
                     I'm afraid to question

                                        it could go in the basement
in the middle of the woods
                        foreign and intriguing

                                        I would try to see every side
would I underanalyze
                what is it doing with me
                                        possess it
would I kill it
                what would it need

                                        I don't want it to confuse me
why do I immediately despise it
                        want to comfort it
                                                kill it

She wanted to cut down all the trees
weird, she was obsessed by their falling
or crushing something like falling, I guess
she didn't like the looks either
of the little pines in a crabby clump
this isn't a joke, she kept saying, they grow too tall
and don't have deep enough roots
to hold this soil at this angle
well it's not your property, but she didn't listen
this isn't a joke, someone must trespass somewhere
illegal or not it's not like I should be in danger
in this state no matter, lines are lines of property
but danger is still danger, and the pines
are dangerous at those angles and this soil, no matter
how unlived-in the property looks, I said
or how bad the situation, some trees got a right
she screamed and ran chattering
up the squirrels, throwing down branches and things
it's a matter of value, she screamed, not just my life
but real value, like the dreams matter as much as fences
like there was really something wrong with this combination
of trees and ground, in that particular pasture which hadn't been used
in so long the pines had taken back the hill like they do
when a spot becomes free like that, especially the white
which don't really tolerate wasted sun and rush to empty it
or fill it, whatever, she said, I'm going to pay this job
until every inch of <u>pine</u> is gone from near this house

hopes up
hopes was up
what you read
when it becomes

clear you are
reading into it

and where you stand
when it becomes clear
you've learned to stand it

or have no standing

mind
the phone you are
told
mind the ringing
or the time
mention
hopes up

slip up
slip next to me and
it will deliver
what's on the mind
slipped on

or out
bite through the
what's to be gotten through

broken bones
don't give the magic
say-so
though it may

obviously hope
it doesn't happen

like it says
in the way you listen up
it never is real

other people
deep as the slope
lacking all types
showing up quickly

endure so long
so long as

distinctions failing
to measure
the books
for comfort
in the chapters

philosophically
measuring the sentence
they hope to sell
off the hope of measuring
the believing

think their
high words topple their roots
successful so you
never notice the difference

or go look up
the difference
in a dictionary

failing pine

or what stops intentions
the firing humiliation
or the silent
smiling beheading

headed up
all about hopes up
and dreams they say
you imagine what's already
coming after
you've imagined it
coming

it's all in your mind
property next door
before you started
seeing it

a psychic can read
into your fears
and make them true
sooner so be sure
only right thinking

hopes grow up in
open abandon

fields nothing
else will take
all hopes too close
together up
only tiny
diameters grow a year
overcrowded

remember to wait

patient
makes a difference
how often the doctor
and the news
arrive

and how the words
will be received
up the chain
the tests up the line
result in the present
conditions

as though anyone
were reading
anything written
in hands
trembling

as though anyone
is thinking about you
when you think of them
or falling
after you

missing you
when you're sleeping

is what they mean
when they say
smiling
how they fell sorry
to have missed you

opens up
hopes up

pretend you've never
intended for anything
to grow there
in such soil at that angle

the impression given
no one paying up
their attention
simple manners overlooked

read into
oracles telling you
what you've just heard
but the no still stands
no when it really says
it matters

what else you do
doesn't matter
they say if your hopes are up
it's better for the future

even if no means no

when you're heading down
nobody hears you
and that's real
when you're under the impression
heading up
still the slightest chance

to stand where there's some standing

on the way down
your mind can tear through
the house to fall
in the bedroom dreaming
the ladder so far up
the ladder it doesn't matter
if you're trespassing

if you're this low
they say you've already
inherited
the view

She says different trees speed
motions not from a hat

She hates the house
she lives in

obsesses
the growing killing
light choking
as quickly as waiting
all there is to know
she finds in no book
except on the state of Maine
the use of pine as boat masts
valued by the king
whenever there was a king
he saved them

they're everywhere
you don't want them the *hats*

the hatred of the house
head bowd
overhead it pines by name
less noise straight
sitting up overhead
she was drawn
feel barely feet up
from her tip roof split
one roof cave
this drawn out timber
over tongue
split the late day
awake and stunn'd
she means fall
to hoist up
five or six men and
other prefalling
conspecifics
the principle of seeing
them first and saving them
for boats the principle
being the first principle
which is the house
and home and hearth to burn
down every inch of shade

"Responsibly" I scratch out some "nerves" (this nervous orderly, from the basement upstairs at midnight) not now, nor have I ever been a responsible worker since "hungrier" is an attribute (he has to clean her light-producing organs) of appetite, these old bodies embroidered in shallow breathing, light having nothing accidentally to do with appetite but with food procurement (tired, less so "consumption") & the electric cord works on sustained static, pitched on carpeted stairs (this porous fabric of old age, as cells slow down) I leave a note for the next guy:

she lies in old sheets

"crewel"

any body shining faintly when taken into a dark room, signifies the dying

the old lady smiled, because I like old ladies and to think of them smiling (he surfs the channels on an old b & w, jerking) a smile one last weapon so I write that *the old lady lies in bed smiling* even as the young man who cares for the night shift (picks his teeth, his guitar) cares more for television & microwave and appliqués simultaneously (leans on the table & thwaps strings against the wooden neck, bending them back) as combustion was once accompanied by heat (the theory fails) though heat alone suffices to illuminate unshelled forms, her clock slows (its display, his percussion) emits some light, placing an emptiness, bedside

or a good-enough vacuum, the three kingdoms of phospherescence: dying animals, vegetables, minerals, or two lumps of sugar struck together

the "shining" deep sea

despite loud guitar she wishes to visit lower settings, slower breathing (rustic antiquity, choppy perhaps: a big amp) or pharmaceutical detail, a pill wave phosphorescence, managing the glow between death beds

for one so aged in fact (in tucked lips, his pick) we've encountered her circuit coiled & solving what he's going to practice tonight, he mutters *changes to soiled sheets*

"crowes"

& she faints into the grief of other self-luminous organisms

holding tighter than she should (her fingers pried from the cord, the steel) as teams redirect wind and solar circuits (feedback bends around him with digits touching, microwaves: a complexity of being turned down) her brittle spine on this occasion (he steps back & drums the tray) after such pressure her inner surface of glass grows mold

& this "glow" accompanies the cessation of animal bodies, marine flesh flashing in dark water, the sustainable energy of anatomical grieving, or a layer-like appearance of lightning in an empty vessel provoked by sparks, red light on her tongue, a mind forfeiting, the digestion waste of hearing and sight through a stained paper gown

"Eat your head, eat your head" candle-bearers of dark, the luminous track (the morning shift just before dawn) in other words, dead fish glowing in the eventual pantry, the mystery of self-luminosity, shit and vomit from eating nothing, still

I like old ladies (across her room, unaware of the short he's caused) their one-pot dinners & smut endured from upcoming generations "to top it all off" (he forks her macaroni with one hand to tweak the volume up again unrecognized) concocting every mealtime, her guide through other cells than suns or bulbs; an ongoing self-battery, weakening

imagine a putrefaction

bearing traces, any body illuminating a doorway, I jot on the chart

is said to behave like the bed-bound, phosphorescent appliances wrapped in
the trunk of an oak, emitting rotting light *she is awake and afraid*

moisture increases it

& the orderlies gets reckless nonetheless, an atmosphere of pure nitrogen,
louder and louder
I say I like her (it doesn't matter either) on mornings which intrude with his
shift's beginning & with the presence of *Noctiluca miliaris*, when I could be
responsible & sing her to sleep, give the kid something else to do (leans
back on the linoleum & turns up reverb) despite the earshot of our charges,
soft-bodied

many of whom are at once self-luminous

she is static electricity I write to forget the significance

a glass rod cloth-handled sparks in her hair, a thin fire, or the decay of
potatoes and their glow (I'll give another example) a diminishing appetite
for movement certain jellyfish float in the current (a hand disturbs the
living water, waking the entire floor) a cacaphony of phospherescence
screaming in semi-private rooms and fallen sheets, sore and scared,
scattering and fading back to dark (arms swing out again just below the
warm water, to shake them up once more) he mounts a chord, up the neck,
two more frets — *this could get us all in trouble*, I write

the nails increase in stench, they turn from matter to trap a sunbeam
a greeting card, flowers on the sill, early anthropology (bare socks pushed
through pile) even sneakers beneath white uniforms imply a crowded
seafloor, hallway the violet end of things where heat is least of all to combine
with ordinary air

her language in sudden arrest and I may further add, to the glow of old ladies

the temperature cooled by removal of final doubts, requires no imagination
to prepare what's left, the body (smiling, in the case of insomnia, insouciant
reverb) an exposure, a shining appearance (the bardo of this to that)
the spark gap

"flier-eyes"

old worms in their nighties with remarkable wattage, despite a few
liquefied pockets, the job of temporary terror, amplified guitar noise,
ancients who have no better name for cobweb-like fungi

Lampyris, she thinks   (and an atmosphere of pure nitrogen)

& imagine a red mushroom with bluish glow, reciprocity of "getting
warm," radiation and absorption, using luminous paint for trains to light
their own tunnels, a fine application of florescence, this orderly duty
scattering waste (the bardo of caring to indifference) or just a broom-swept
hallway

uprooted and isolated, many nights a self-lighted closet
full of diamonds and lime, luminous on their own after isolation

"crewel"

reaching of the body's molecules, results (his strumming, beating air against
it, or the bath of sound waves) in the strong glow of oyster shells in pitch
dark coves

(and would it help to quit this job, or fire any of these punks?) I leave a
note to ease our minimum wage, the constant turnover, I leave *a smile at
the crummy sheets* shift by shift, piled by the door.

lights up

(a motion)
CAPTURED
           (FLIGHT)
overlapping
(SENSED)

      BLACKOUT (*well lit*)

SCENE: TESSELLATION

Tessella becomes a character! (*she thinks*)
congruence: a Shape
All that isn't her is someone else! What she is isn't anyone!

        centerstage
        (she thinks)
(A Shape)

    Tessella explains her innermost feelings
  Tessella examines her senses   *her past*

      CAPTURED

    Tessella approaches fate cautiously
  Tessella's actions begin to contradict themselves (Shapes*)*
      she adjusts, abutted
    Tessella regards her life compared to others

(Action)
SENSED

      (Shapes abutting Shape)
      CAPTURED

that individuals live mosaically
that free-living wild animals don't stand in silhouette
against man-shaped backgrounds

    that prison cells do not overlap *(the fighting!)*
    that at the end of individuals: *(individuals!)*

    that we think thinking stays congruent with thinking
    each species to its world a mere technical mimicry

    ours for minds under overarching regimes
    ours for the identity of numbers

    profiting from parking lots and busy streets, a weedy chorus
    migrates in planes corresponding to stereotypes, pacing
    at thirty thousand feet to avoid more fighting
    the freedom to live by fixed design
    eating from plastic pans to ingest an in-flight meal
    playing hands of limited fortune
    we slip from country to country
    to be touched, to be fed, to travel the given distance
    as entertainment shopping supreme arch-enemies
    jumping from species to species
    to digest
    new interface metaphors

        arching, Tessella profiles perfectly into the
        outline of an enemy (she thinks)

(she senses)   *(furnishes her house)*
her way through danger   resumes   *(she thinks)*

    startled   *she notices*   an Archway

(a Shape)

Surveilled
an untamed creature, congruent with her outline
seamless with her thinking   everything she isn't
just at the hard edge of her border
any motion inside her house expands the notion
of enemy and house   to include this terror
adjusting for the spill of her own body temperature

(a motion)
DETECTED

someone else in the infrared night
prey for her, or prey for her enemy

a motion
CAPTURED

flight

blackout (WELL LIT)

(SHAPE)

(A shape's negative shape)

Tessella regaining her sense of her house
tethered point by point
to a grammar of space-time

testing for intelligence with the use of mirrors
persecuted by fears of identity theft
making a responsive environment from emergent sensors
total output dumping information
with feeling
with feedback algorithms

(an *action*)
SENSED

thus purveying protection, handlers manipulate
psychic distances, the nodes of the sensors carefully correlated

eye to eye/hand to   hand/street to street
dopplar radars, lasers, GPS beacons
peer where peerlessness dwells
the crowd, the thicket, children's games
dense in unwarranted privacy

       Tessella assumes the central encryption
in the roar of secrets

       a night moth deaf to everything but one species of bat
            her own congruent enemy
       its chirp the only sound she hears in an otherwise silent world

"I went to create a web domain but someone had created it"
"I went to become an individual but everyone had become it"

(A Shape)   *(a motion)*
                                     CAPTURED

       Tessella dreams of sharing strong feelings
       but can't sound out her own name

       an acrid narrowing of life around its entire perimeter

                         TESSELLATION

BLACKOUT *(fully lit)*

SCENE: CRITICAL DISTANCES

Then we borrow him from him:

                     (A Shape)
                     PLACE-MARKED

     H. Hediger (1908-1992)

historical action-figure
old individual of the heroic class
harboring biography, reinforced by a chorus
protagonist of his adventure, setting out
as zoo-director, chance observer
rearranger of scattered and unpretentious tesserae
surveilled non-human gestures of suffering
marked on pages

(*sense*)
SENSED

gesture
CAPTURED
actogram as negative of gesture
CAPTURED

his work at the height of the zoological garden
earned him a reputation

MOTION
sensed

          bystanding luxuriously
          a man of extreme empathy
          practically lingering
    inside animals   like a burglar picks his way
    through treasures of intimacy
          crowding the terrain with concepts
          of autonomy
          or piloting small planes at higher purposes
          over unfiltered wilderness
          locating last remains, looking down
          jungles   tundras   deserts
          a few sentient beings fleeing along the borders
                    of human charity
          landscaped with technological features

since it's easier to invent life-like animations
back at the office in bullet lists
for wholesale or home use, rather than track unruly noise
down through clouds of individual minds

(carnivore-eyes fix forward
jaws just behind)

MOTION
sensed

(herbivores stand horizontal-eyed
split axes scan the scene, their non-overlapping vision

shaped from escape pressure)

centerstage   (she thinks)
Tessella scans this pale H.Hediger

entering her story   skims "world history"
image-archives of local programming, amplified

LIGHTS WAY UP (*BLACKOUT*)

SCENE: A SHAPE

(a Shape)   she flinches in fear   her own desires
managed through all-deceiving surfaces
programmed to cues of beauty
her hair sheened and untangled
conspicuous through elaborate domestication
and the lack of constant battle
to be insatiable, conditioned at the code-layer
for several generations   a housing complex
surrounded by open space, the greenbelt
her psychotrope

she gets a good start from the bathroom
to the kitchen   to the bed
scavenging domestic energy in the spatial separation of body functions,
a fully built-out stage set, a planet-park
                    insomniac, orgiastic with confessional monotony

MOTION
captured   *motion*
                    SENSED

                    a captive wild lion enacts
     a preliminary fight response   *finger-tripped*
               a wave of paw   *a Snarl*
               the tamer controlling every move
with his smallest gestures

                              (a Shape)
                              FIXED

as flight is cornered into a sudden attack
                    (Shape's negative Shape)
the critical distance doled out in centimeters
before the tiger leaps one stool over
          provoked by a step back and a whip snap
effigy of fear in the never changing escape-scape
of mortal enemies

Thus *H.Hediger* collected behavior
from forests not yet stored as data
conjectured, the old lover's library
groped at the threshold of animal minds
like lofty caverns, their behaviors
bound up in words after the fact of them
or in love with the outline of ideas, congruent antitheses

"access to which will some day be granted"
or one way to make murder sound not too unreasonable
in euphemism, biography's sooty mirror

now captivated by this domestic scene, *H. Hediger*
overheard in history   might forget himself
or find sanctuary in conspicuous hair
the overcooked human packaging of the 21st century

      Tessella! I am this character you can love   or kill
      for exactly what I do and say   *my totality*
      coarsely, an insight   that you are captive
      and untame   for how close I can come without

      touching   *(she thinks)*
                 how dangerous it all can *feel unfamiliar*
      and you recoil across yourself
as though distrustful that in this rendition I am possessed of
sympathetic understanding   *and other useless skills*

               (a motion)
               SENSED

      (motion)
      FIXED

I am everything that also is not me
overstepping myself across my overlapping

      Tessella groans
      implying something preemptive

      (motion)
      CAPTURED

               (senses)
               MARKED

H. Hediger overhead in a private plane

  trigger ready   *(helping out)*
a wild grizzly sow crossing rough tundra   in another eye
sight *a monkey   a tranquilizer dart right into an elk*
a female lynx   dying of starvation, relocatable
lifting off, *a moose wrapped in a sling*
        fixed with radio transmitters
 compassionate fantasy of acceptable casualties
cracks like buckshot   numbers rounded up
minutes later *(fatal terror)*
                darting and dropping H.Hediger (watching)
                a marksman and aid workers waiting
as a tranquilized elk panics into a raging creek
        where normally strong it flails
 head slips too heavy   too drugged it can't find footing
        and in familiar water drowns

                motion
                SENSED

in the same way the conspicuous songs of birds
allow safer passages, flying fast and far
above the grunts and growls of forest creatures
calling fatal attention to themselves
even during the cabin service
        risking the small itinerary
to get fresh water or in-flight snack
if you're lucky
the right to move to the bathroom or recline
in an assigned seat where one might sneak a nap

(she thinks)

Repose, stroke   H.Hediger   touch her?
all that is recognizably him doesn't fly at a woman's approach
            tamed, he doesn't flinch
a gesture responsive to a human Shape   *she would arouse*
            a shadow passing along a path
                    to indicate his private plane overhead
garbled speech outside the cage
dreaming the flight distance down to nothing

            or touch him?
                an enemy par excellence
(she thinks)
                despite a total extinguishing of prior overlapping
                in which whole networks of lives got muddy
                    in shocks of unexpected meeting
                not to be confused with programs of domestication
                her hyperactive coarseness and   (pacing)
                    her small ears, and delicate jaw

            MEMORY
            sensed

Tessella considers this novel adjacency
            all that is not her   *and one H.Hediger*

            the critical distance between competitors
up for grabs when conspecifics pass too close
                whereas *the fox and the badger share their fields*
                and male swans allow grebes, coots and gulls
but never another swan
tracking across the big blue sky
                jumbo jets at the price of the neighborhood only
euphemistically called "love"   for rituals of tolerance
            adorned with concepts to keep us toying with it
                    (*quick, interrupting*)   a picture window

entire bodies evolve to 'beauty' from pressures of enemies and
how they act   taking special shapes for certain audiences
      Tessella's seduction entirely pre-prepared for me
by me

            a position
            FIXED

    an animal identifying herself with her house or just the relief
of a first-class seat

            fitted
            to its place

      like some creatures literally turn
      their bodies into homes
      with faces shut like doors

      the other tranquilized elk staggers to the woods and
pitching headfirst into loam, suffocates under his own weight

          POINT
          fixed

working a classified job
bearing samples to a warehouse in Colorado
where we met at a conference of data specialists
thinking *life is a matter of degree*
and death stays very much alive
until all information becomes nonsense
a mangled silence just beyond the cell's reproductive potential

(*motion*)
CAPTURED

(POINT)

fixed

TURN

she thinks (spatially)

one special moment between us
could be congruent with the overall project
of overarching   (*not too close*)
a rest restored only as the enemy backs away

centerstage *(she thinks)*

my own house is safe

watching weakly

Tessella considers the nature of furniture

the nature we have now, desiring support

for what we remember we possessed in other forms

relieved of impermanence

reinvesting the dividends of death
in skin which belies the math of the non-linear
storytelling of the crowd

Tessella crawls to the couch

relieved no one else is there

occupies   time   staring at the books
this historical Hediger until finally she can love no one else
the rare beauty of secluded exclusive properties
picture windows onto adjacent events, remote actions
up close
Reposed in her becoming
(*a pose*)
Re   *a very congruent act of abutting*

teasing toward a new lover

her data craves observing

Refined, outlined her flight muscle

aroused   chronic, hyperactive
              to occupy herself
              in the ways Men occupy Men   (she thinks)
    spatially   *what do women occupy worldwide*
except some categories, enemy to even a small colony of ants
                immobilizing, tranquil
       minds preoccupied   by every flying thing

SCENE: EVERYTHING

(she gestures illegibly)   to log a vital bit of time, uncaptured
          a beast passing purely unrendered
or behave as they always have
                            she comes a tiny bit closer
(another gesture, beyond anything)   in a world which no
longer coheres or responds   *the dance form evolves*
              suddenly
imagining worlds without living creatures in them
Galileo dreamt   *a few impotent movements*
        some simple mosaic in which living spaces of
individual species don't cross   *except, I remark*
tessellations only occur in *artificial conditions*
        like fences and money and streets and police
        (she motions to the familiar, *yes*) dividing what's
private and invisible (home, territories, love) into property

(I smile, not really a wave but a gesture cute with language)
while *(she thinks)* the remoter the connection between the
animals, the more territory overlaps
                            (it's true *I wave again*)
       motion
       SENSED

that home forms the basis of the whole living system

motion
CAPTURED

the captive wild animal's manmade life, a neighborhood
association   *wondering what I would say to that*
she pauses

                              (Posing)
                              CAPTURED

                    circles from the kitchen to the bookshelf
she gestures toward the foodtray
              some undulating movement of the whole body
congruent and formed from its stimulus
              my approach now seeming fairly obvious
and aware that critical responses always aim toward the enemy in
one direction *I make an inverse shape to hers*

                              an action
                              SENSED

revealing subtle differences between *H.Hediger* and other
imaginary characters, my insistence on the investigation of
behavior   *plus*   sympathetic understanding

              her undulating becomes more pronounced
              perched on the arm of the couch

              I sort of wave again (noisily)

the original escape response of all vertebrates, cornered
              she shuts me down   and my library of old books
the symptom of being such a larger animal
haunted by the narrow ceiling
airspace, vocal range, diminishing

SCENE: TRIGGERS

H. Hediger and Tessella on Abutting Lawn

two characters   lacking overlap

falling silent   *adjacent, their arms entwining*
        inverting patterns   *what isn't her*
             becomes him
         stomach hollowed   *back*   *heads together*
neither one more than breathing   *she could dance*
until the slightest   *hand movement*
      (thinking)   *movement*   *sends her darting*
 to the next room
a safer place to watch
what might have happened

(a *motion*)
SENSED   *gestures*
                   FIXED

unsustainable ideals, these zoo cells
abutting, relieved of survival
puts us into heat
to avoid fighting we must be quickly separated
and entertained remotely
the original violence concealed
conceptually or literally
in dances more or less ready always
for flight   [THWARTED]

        maybe we kissed, desperately
        or tenderly watched ourselves

        out of habit

(his: *out of print*)　　TRIGGERS

(hers: *out of character*)　　　TRIGGERS

telling this story which began before birth

while Hediger famously watched zoo-keepers
psyche-out the inmates with excessive petting
killing with a kindness as unbearable as direct flame
the keepers' self-love of love
a revolting and deadly obsession with touching
the worst possible torture
within the general overarching torture

ZOO ANIMALS, TRIGGERED (A BULLETED LIST)

- overheated by direct sunshine within minutes

- overexposed without places to hide from being seen

- stuffed on diseased fatty foods from the sick hands of children

- spiteful adoration in which no critical reaction is possible

- a fatal show of raw animal

- the mention of compulsory sharing of living quarters

- despite all the gadgetry, wireless, circuitry

- designed to trace or encrypt the sensor network (*motion*)

- scavenge mostly irrelevant energies

- to draw seemingly infinite bodies of knowledge

- while budgeting to maintain only a few live examples

- in the "Stay" of domesticated use

- any new interest makes morbid hypertrophic fixation on single
  things like boxes
- doors
- food
- begging

an action
FIXED   AN ACTION
           fixed

before the information
we just didn't know, we said
we just didn't know how many
old habits make the world inhabitable
we just didn't know
how many were out there
beside us
in the conditioned darkness of stage light

BLACKOUT
(*infrared*)

SCENE: MINUS THE BEAR

when the skeleton and fur, bones, skin are gone
the collar remains signaling in the tundra
chasing down the beacon, they find even the most outdated
technology outlives an overstressed life

"I went to make a statement, but everyone had made it"
"I went to live marginally, but everyone had lived it"

one tangling endless drama and we're centered in it
and we're never it

MOVEMENT

(sensed)

MOTION
(rendered)

from the ground or through the air
a low level electromagnetic pulse
makes motion transmit heat
like the sun visible through the airplane window
packed arm to arm we fall asleep
while watching familiar movies across the long-haul
like particles of dung or glandular scent
trace our detachable stories

you can't write because it's already written
your hands cannot move, they move
triggered, they are captured
they cannot move, they're all that move

we borrow *H.Hediger* in a cruising altitude —
this being where zoo-keeping has placed its discoverers
zoo air-to-ground, zoo-binocular, zoo before the fog

the arctic Scoters implanted with satellite transmitters
        keep to themselves; once-touched by our scent
they stay outcast or for the sake of the group won't
                contaminate the rest
                easy pickings for predators, dead in a week

the purpose of the ideal cage of course
   to make the inmate convinced that the cage is precisely
the same size as its territory, remove the friction
of conspecifics or hostile species
almost but not quite nullifying the need for vocabulary
   attention dimmed quasi-consensually
   into an affluent gloom of peace
where the young realize there's not much to grow old for
   except growing older
an endless old age beginning younger and younger

     heat
     TRIGGERED

possums will kill themselves jumping at the ceiling
I turn to Tessella
framed at the picture window
    crushing figure-eights against the wall
    focal points at the door and foodtray

  she keeps insisting on the food tray
  (like I might relax enough to eat)
  a dangerously inactive hyperactivity

(*motion*)
SENSED   SHAPE
           (*negative shape*)

only tameness, if achieved, is calming, finally
the suffering wild animal resigns
to the stink of the enemy's hands
on everything
Tessella could succumb
to the quiet summer evening
the pleasure of which is a near-death paralysis
a few last private breaths

SCENE: BLAME OURSELVES

it was the function of the chorus to know what the hero was
thinking, the chorus making no sense itself, no history
and yet nowadays it's heroes everywhere
sitting on stoops, making nothing happen
even when the chorus reveals
it's all chorus who will face the decisions
how can choruses make decisions, we wonder
wailing and lamenting stupid things on television
the scattered echoes of true horrors
somehow beyond the nodes of information
officially unheard-of

So I told her   *(looking the other way)*

" *if a socially lower-ranking animal is tyrannized by the others*
 to an exaggerated degree through confined space under
 conditions of captivity it will be left literally without room or
 food. Before succumbing it will perhaps try to resist this
 unbearable state of affairs and perish in the ensuing battle"

Tess moves almost to my throat   *(touch her?)*

                    going on about how *money* doesn't overlap
its perfect shapes   and negative shapes
compare everyone's bank accounts   *she flairs*

                    and wives and children are possessed
in specific non-overlapping quantities   *(she thinks)*
                              and later *she wants to talk*
and everything gets really overarticulated
in loops of thoughts and I quote
"to make some sense, make some drinks"

while we overhear a wasp
trapped between windows
our bodies adjust to the horrible knocking

motion
SENSED

a new and exclusive community
defending against newer enemies
uncaptured   but captured
between our windows
beneath our clothing

SCENE: A SERIES OF PAUSES ALONG THE EARTH

sanitizing conflicts we deploy
a million forms of euphemism
Tessella, Hediger
adjacent characters   ongoing imprecisions

Tessella, *from the other room*, makes the slightest movement
I read the mark on a kymograph, every change in her center of
gravity   *she ponders the future, our characters*
something like ships at night

(a *motion*)
SENSED

the information safe between ten-foot walls
climate controlled, military security, windowless
the data stares into nothing
architects of a frozen future
the most essential real property (DNA)

the last stronghold of species
falling down the ladder

Tessella regards her potential as mate-material
    clocking evolutionary pressure (she thinks)
(she feels)   the pinch of unfelt organs
        overfelt she feels them again

        (adjusting her organs) Tessella compares herself to her
memory a few days before she met me

a million monarchs died in Mexico this morning
addresses miscorresponded to addressees
weather's responsive filtering
within the species' house, homes grew invisible
to the outside eye, just a series of pauses along the earth
        later to identify death, reprogrammable and cleaned
        like bodies being cared for in empires of English

BLACKOUT *(lights up)*

SCENE: SCENE

Tessella's smell captures my senses
    remotely I remember a kiss
the visual territory, too
of a face, landscaped
reminds me of my own interior

    (thinking of her *thinking)*

        territories of distinct creatures
            staying out of each other's hair

Tessella's hair shakes but I cannot touch it

(my own hand moves the pointer)

she doesn't like to have her hair touched
in the act of making love   or even thinking about it

motion
DETECTED

most species' territories contain reliable points for *feeding,
storing, refuge, bathing, wallowing, looking-out, defecating,
dismembering, drinking, scent marking, scratching, child-
rearing, loving* all the different specific home-places which
mark the comforting centers of a life worth living

lights up
BLACKOUT

but should I, from this height, forget Tessella's
insistence that clothing also makes the man, *it is only
me laughing*   to myself, the tiny fact that so many
animals hate the color white
     white clothes, white patches, white walls
and that they die from symptoms of glare
each fresh strength depleted by a new exhaustion

lights up
BLACKOUT

the species hovering above each carcass
like a zebra shading her foal
death like a mother animal can only protect
with darkness and shadows

111

the considerable relationship one has to home
as impossible to measure as love or fear

Tessella rejects my ferocious argument
her display consisting of tooth and claw, ritually
again and again, and promises of skin
now a singular form of torment
producing gambits of learned helplessness
I remind her *the journey takes some months*
to the farther reaches of the Arctic
where the she-bear won't take it easily and there may be blood

lights up
BLACKOUT

that we're at the end of individuals *(she thinks)*
that we can't bear our own kind on top of us
            but tolerate a stray cat, birds and flies
like the thought of a stranger in the room makes her stiffen
though she enjoys bluejays in the yard
            an unexpected smile escapes

A MOTION
sensed

as an agile user controls the screen
knows how to swoop down, grab
finger-triggered objects *from any array*
            H. Hediger not quite myself
in the strange fraction delay
between finger stroke and image response
                        (rotate, pan or zoom)
            multiple degrees of freedom
        influencing her shy glance

                                her leg pulled back
                                    calculable, virtual

                                            an action
                                            CAPTURED

the basic set of simple operations
providing the widest range of possible content
whereas she finally indicates
that there are thirty of me in the phone book
        I think
        only thirty?   *It's a small number . . .*

                    LIGHTS UP
                    infrared

and it's piles of carcasses all over Europe
and again there's a wasp at the window
parsing at the level of perception
this or that historical body
as coarse in grain as Tessella, loyal to noncompressability
and a certain belief in the possibilities of encryption
we remain, after all, merely poetry
at a hyperactive pace preventing sleep
despite tentative gestures through complexity barriers

                    (a motion)
                    CAPTURED

and still it's cow legs in the air, mass graves, the smell of burnt
skin, it's legs and stomachs and teeth all over again
a series of changes too complex to repeat
killed for being fed our own heads

SCENE: MONKEY HOUSE

inaudible from the monkey houses

monkey paradises high monkey terraces

the monkey　　　*drugged into a black-out*

wakes
FIXED

the new world *he considers*
the house-cage features
or maybe he was bred in captivity?
and birth (he thinks) *was the blackout?*
he doesn't remember
the barrier he could cross backward
he doesn't remember getting here
so he presumes this natural disaster
must be singular

touches
WALLS　　　　*touching*
　　　　　　　BARS

　　　　　　　　　　　he discovers walls
bars, bones, cells, blood and water
his attention hardens and worse, convincing
like nights broken by fleeting food-seasons
and visitor-seasons, and time which once flowed freely weighs
down the floor, the food, some toys, captivating

captured
IMAGINATION

restlessly he fixates on the drain
for such a tree-climber relies on spaces
                            into which they cannot see
the tree-canopy offering a shadowy void
where shit falls fast and out of sight
but in the cage stays visible, strangely over-imaginable
                            in a confining morbid fascination
an exaggeration preoccupied with under-occupation
            instead of disappearing now the shit's There
in the fully lit indiscretion of concrete
                    the monkey cannot detach himself
            from alarm, sleep or confusion
and in all the entertaining dreams
                    this is my favorite window, that is where the
            food comes, I hate that one perch, I like that water
            trough, I love this chair, this window, that handler
every area of the cage soaked in endless feelings

before the information
we just didn't know, we said
we just didn't know

                            (lights up)
                            DARKNESS

SCENE: FULL BUILD-OUT

in dribs and drabs the chorus makes some decisions
standing forlorn in open meadow, staring pathetically
at dramas which look nothing like decisions
at tragedies escaping notice
mocked from all sides
unable to find the undisturbed play of animals or children
the chorus laments the imagination like a stay of execution
the charity of isolated parks on which all animals depend

at the center of the stage
        Tess considers the tamer's ring and practical
     manipulations of distance
         how to get
         him here
         beside her

by using his fear   *(a motion)* CAPTURE
by extension   her fear   SHE THINKS
     (A Shape)   abuts, retreats
    (negative outline of Shape)

prompted by the deafening noise
I go get a glass and a book
and trap the wasp against the sill, remove him
outside to some other end beyond our control *(we think)*
our motions as unperceived as fate itself
      and Tessella would say I'm silly
       for this wasp-relocation effort
        but she's distracted through it

       (an action)
       SENSED   *(reaction)*
                      CAPTURED

given free movement, animals separate
steadying conflicts, avoiding final solutions
but in captivity the only resolution comes
by eliminating rivals completely
in the scarcity of space, excessive density incites
bad behavior toward single individuals
too abstract   *to stop the hand*   *to stop the mind*
unless you love one, I suppose
       or one was your mother

for the fifth time tonight, Tess shrugs off my affection
            as child's play   a touch too easy

reminding me that capturing minds
                not territories   not bodies
is the real glory, remake dreams, confiscate thoughts
and keepers of this zoo-logic require subtler training
                new forms of writing
                more interactive, user-friendly   never forced

                                        a motion
                                        CAPTURED

                    adjusting the meaning of the word, not its forms
                    adjusting the distance between house and home
                    which is not congruent with environment
                    but scene   though in practice it's impossible
                                to fit the cages
                    exactly to the flight distance of every animal
                    so the answer is still to make the flight
                                fit the cage
reduce the captive's response to touch
so if she can't get far enough away from you
                                she won't die of it

                    SCENE: SELF SACRIFICING

before the trigger-fingers

                    SPEECH
                    recognized

language cleans the situation in after-effects
        (she thinks)   vestigial sense organs wired together

to communicate spatially emancipated
after all the suggestion of *touch*
Tessella suggests we now forget
         "H. Hediger"
(she thinks)   (that's sentimental)
               (I swallow a cough)
ignoring the obvious human interest of the story
      we've got other examples of rare species
      I reassure her, our zoos compete
      we like to say, with extinction
collecting specimens like ruined civilizations
from overhead Hediger dangles his private plane
brush forests, swamps, jungles, coastal cliffs, rainforest
over a hand-stitched road someone draws a dart-gun

      the old-fashioned kind of hero ambles on
      "old bears" they're called
      a celebrated ferocity, that grizzled silver look
           Hediger's got it, and the notebook
a special assignment, uneasy about the subject
resorting to writing a kind of novel
and if there were another scene   *there'd be turbulence*
of the prop-plane kind   *and a series of short drops*
indicating we'll be landing sooner than expected
       in the bear sow's longest known sleep
       for which we invented the EKG
       for sleep's secret *mission in progress*
     like the elephants', once mysterious
     so lightly balanced on their feet
     they'd wake and trumpet at any approach
     while tonight our filters observe them whole
     and for sleep so for hibernation
the canopy opens, the parting grass, the cave reveals
       the hero adjacent to the immobilized subject

hovering lightly   running nerveless power
all we know about her brain reveals
this bear is just a passing shadow
branching in the sleep of death
still slightly tricky to light unaccounted-for consciousness
                on the ground now
I guide my hands to the sensation of a beast; I guide the collar
to its most cowardly place; I guide the half-conscious head
away, not to avoid me or for an instant think that I won't kill her,
my human threat my only shield, a power asymmetry
keeping me alive, her fear my last defense
against one middle-aged female grizzly
her cubs shrieking a few hundred yards back

     I recall Tessella saying not to bother
     with all that life-saving swashbuckling
     self-sacrificing over anything that isn't me
     isn't me to worry over

                and what's a trained zoologist to do with
           that but go make another drink?

           motion
           SENSED

I could make perfect observations about her and the grizzlies
because I'm practiced in the art of perfect observations
and so pretty terrible at it

Tessella continues to defend herself like some *individual*
despite the coarse rub of evidence — and this while I'm going to
a hero's death   or at least an emergency landing against
the backdrop   I wish for death suddenly   like a mania driving
me to it   a smaller version of a polar bear in captivity

at one-millionth its natural range languishing over a
meaningless work-out   some movable net of empathy
pulls me on, some source of distance   beyond which
mania piles on mania   and here we are sinking in it   wanting
death because it's a cowards way   not to actually look at it

SCENE: USER FRIENDLY

so the plane lands only to take off again
and for a few loud minutes everything's planes
this grizzly mom pulled from the den
in the course of sleep finds no winter
but a cage in the cargo hold
            a collective action accumulating to me
justified with nonsense   *a cage without her cubs*
                    a skidding halt
human faces disgust me, I write
                        but mine is most disgusting?

                looking
                ASKANCE

the approach of a contact-animal to a distance-animal
can be brutal as they each defend (misunderstand)
unfamiliar language
                & as though she'd never been afraid
                she leans up for a second kiss
                a second-thought
                underhandedly suppressed
Tessella's hypersexuality, and mine
signs of our domestication, get really ugly
stereotyped against a blur of breeding seasons
we gesture more frantically

and even my use of animal behavior
to thwart her eternal vigilance should constitute treason
a selfish inexcusable melodrama
in a captivity where social contacts only intensify
without the possibility of avoidance between exits
excuse me while I kill myself

> *pointlessness*
> FIXED
>
> > *inaction*
> > SENSED

as zoos get upgraded with scented toys
and other props, artificial snowbanks and "real" carcasses
eliciting new repertoire and better performances
for the captive audience
and still the keepers wonder why hiding remains most
critical to the survival of the animals

> (a Shape)
> *imagined*

to be tamed is not simply a clash of loyalties
    she slowly twists her wrist, the glass, her gaze
    a conflict between necessity and memory
a fold into the space between us
    anchored somehow in accident and intimacy

(a Shape)
outline/outline
enemy/enemy
        it's like she's caught dead
before being caught
except I'm the historical member around here

of the set: {H. Hediger}
and I ask how many species have died out, rhetorically
simply through over-attachment to home, or food
or some other intensely felt reason not to run away

SCENE: DR. MOREAU'S ISLAND

(sets and lights)
the protagonist overpopulates
like a view from the plane, wild and narrowing
nothing but generations, artificially isolated
the chorus heroically adjusting
to the meaninglessness of motion sickness
potent with communication

(flash)
POINT

keepers learn never to chase an escaped animal
go around, get ahead, cut her off
slow her down, remind her who you are
                    if you are someone she knows
                    act even more knowing
not that it matters now, but I did in fact with a tape measure
measure hundreds of actual flight distances
in hundreds of specific cases
and made comprehensive records

escape
SIGNAL

survival through distance is our planet's inheritance
using it up too quickly we slip
to the nearest habitable get-away

which is why cage breakers will always win
over electrical barriers, thermal barriers
bars and mesh, water or death
the deepest pit won't stop a captive wild herd
running from man's curious face
>   *I float my hands up and down*
>   *calling for calm*
the universal enemy of all animals in the free state
their lives exhausting themselves searching
for somewhere flight isn't totally absurd

>   *(a gesture)*
>   CAPTURED

(a motion)
SENSED

actions round off and shorten, blunt and fix
sure signs of bad treatment
>   *See, we're distracted*
(I think)
>   *(she thinks)*

even the biggest apes can be moved
through tiny "shocks"
position the body through micro-adjustments in flight response

>   *tiny glimpses of snakes and turtles*

the crowd disperses into a fog of chorus
perceiving the largesse of its gifts, thanking itself
choking its heart on smoggy thoughts
disharmonious moods, backs into a mob
for some last-ditch isolation
>   *which is perhaps why I finally assure Tessella I won't*

return   anytime soon
        the non-return a subtler escape-form

but before I finish that thought, my bear sow dies
of "capture myopathy"
her muscles wasted and boiling from the heat of chase
and handling

            (Pose)
Re-pose
ALERT

and still from this height all feels manageable:
                the example of the she-bear
                dead to her cubs and to herself
remains quite informative, her own cells
may guarantee something like her species
despite the inevitable absence of specific wild members

            centerstage   *(she thinks, willfully)*

    lights up!
    lights up!

            Tessella examines the situation
flapping her wings in a Leerlauf response

H. Hediger throws one last glimpse through the picture window
        hunger and love can be postponed   *(he thinks)*

            she flaps and flaps
            as though expecting to fly
    because she would be relieved to fly
        if only an enemy would ever really show up

but until then, she frantically exaggerates the terror
of ordinary things

everything that's me is something else *(he thinks)*
that is, there's nothing carved from everything

    even Tessella's neighborhood shows
        sparrows, rats, pigeons, wasps
    foraging backyards and parking lots, the few creatures
profiting from industrial abundance
        an Escher-world of animal technophiles
    paying dearly for life on Moreau's island

    the shape of her arm extends
    into the profile of a soaring bird
cooked out, watched out, hunted out, tamed
        perfecting a human theology
the subtraction of sanity and privacy

        CAPTURED
        (a motion)

           (a Shape)
           SENSED

BLACKOUT (LIGHTS UP)

the chorus augments again
lamenting their noise, lamenting their heroes
that at the end, individuals
overlapping, fighting

    swallowing all the hiding places
    of animals and children

"But,"
we ask,
"what children?"

congruent to my sympathies
Tessella compares herself to others
examines the past, her senses
a fly arising inside the picture window
starts to move, slowly opening her hand
she goes to kill it
I trace a pattern along her palm
just once to take her time, to overlap

(a motion)

FELT

just this once

pour out your heart
don't put all the animal out

New Directions Paperbooks—A Partial Listing

For a complete listing request free catalog from New Directions, 80 Eighth Avenue,
New York 10011; or visit our website, www.ndpublishing.com

†Bilingual

Miroslav Krleža, *On the Edge of Reason*. NDP810.
Shimpei Kusano, *Asking Myself/Answering Myself*. NDP566.
Davide Lajolo, *An Absurd Vice*. NDP545.
P. Lal, ed., *Great Sanskrit Plays*. NDP142.
Tommaso Landolfi, *Gogol's Wife*. NDP155.
James Laughlin, *The Love Poems*, NDP865.
  Poems New and Selected. NDP857.
Comte de Lautréamont, *Maldoror*. NDP207.
D.H. Lawrence, *Quetzalcoatl*. NDP864.
Irving Layton, *Selected Poems*. NDP431.
Christine Lehner, *Expecting*. NDP572.
Siegfried Lenz, *The German Lesson*. NDP618.
Denise Levertov, *The Life Around Us*. NDP843.
  Selected Poems. NDP968.
  The Stream and the Sapphire. NDP844.
  This Great Unknowing. NDP910.
Li Ch'ing-Chao, *Complete Poems*. NDP492.
Li Po, *The Selected Poems*. NDP823.
Enrique Lihn, *The Dark Room*.† NDP452.
Clarice Lispector, *The Hour of the Star*. NDP733.
  Near to the Wild Heart. NDP698.
  Soulstorm. NDP671.
Luljeta Lleshanaku, *Fresco*. NDP941.
Federico García Lorca, *The Cricket Sings*.† NDP506.
  Five Plays. NDP506.
  In Search of Duende.† NDP858.
  Selected Letters. NDP557.
  Selected Poems.† NDP114.
Xavier de Maistre,*Voyage Around My Room*. NDP791.
Stéphane Mallarmé, *Mallarmé in Prose*. NDP904.
  Selected Poetry and Prose.† NDP529.
Oscar Mandel, *The Book of Elaborations*. NDP643.
Abby Mann, *Judgment at Nuremberg*. NDP950.
Javier Marías, *All Souls*. NDP905.
  A Heart So White. NDP937.
  Tomorrow in the Battle Think On Me. NDP923.
Bernadette Mayer, *A Bernadette Mayer Reader*. NDP739.
Michael McClure, *Rain Mirror*. NDP887.
Carson McCullers, *The Member of the Wedding*. NDP394.
Thomas Merton, *Bread in the Wilderness*. NDP840.
  Gandhi on Non-Violence. NDP197.
  New Seeds of Contemplation. NDP337.
  Thoughts on the East. NDP802.
Henri Michaux, *Ideograms in China*. NDP929.
  Selected Writings.† NDP263.
Henry Miller, *The Air-Conditioned Nightmare*. NDP587.
  The Henry Miller Reader. NDP269.
  Into the Heart of Life. NDP728.
Yukio Mishima, *Confessions of a Mask*. NDP253.
  Death in Midsummer. NDP215.
Frédéric Mistral, *The Memoirs*. NDP632.
Eugenio Montale, *Selected Poems*.† NDP193.
Paul Morand, *Fancy Goods* (tr. by Ezra Pound). NDP567.
Vladimir Nabokov, *Laughter in the Dark*. NDP729.
  Nikolai Gogol. NDP78.
  The Real Life of Sebastian Knight. NDP432.
Pablo Neruda, *The Captain's Verses*.† NDP345.
  Residence on Earth,† NDP340.
Robert Nichols, *Arrival*. NDP437.
Charles Olson, *Selected Writings*. NDP231.
Toby Olson, *Human Nature*. NDP897.
George Oppen, *Selected Poems*. NDP970.
Wilfred Owen, *Collected Poems*. NDP210.
José Pacheco, *Battles in the Desert*. NDP637.
Michael Palmer, *Codes Appearing*. NDP914.
  The Promises of Glass. NDP922.
Nicanor Parra, *Antipoems: New and Selected*. NDP603.
Boris Pasternak, *Safe Conduct*. NDP77.
Kenneth Patchen, *Memoirs of a Shy Pornographer*. NDP879.
Octavio Paz, *The Collected Poems*.† NDP719.
  Sunstone.† NDP735.
  A Tale of Two Gardens: Poems from India. NDP841.
Victor Pelevin, *Omon Ra*. NDP851.
  A Werewolf Problem in Central Russia. NDP959.
  The Yellow Arrow. NDP845.
Saint-John Perse, *Selected Poems*.† NDP547.
Po Chü-i, *The Selected Poems*. NDP880.
Ezra Pound, *ABC of Reading*. NDP89.
  Confucius.† NDP285.
  Confucius to Cummings. NDP126.

A Draft of XXX Cantos. NDP690.
  The Pisan Cantos. NDP977.
Caradog Prichard, *One Moonlit Night*. NDP835.
Qian Zhongshu, *Fortress Besieged*. NDP966.
Raymond Queneau, *The Blue Flowers*. NDP595.
  Exercises in Style. NDP513.
Margaret Randall, *Part of the Solution*. NDP350.
Raja Rao, *Kanthapura*. NDP224.
Herbert Read, *The Green Child*. NDP208.
Kenneth Rexroth, *Classics Revisited*. NDP621.
  100 Poems from the Chinese. NDP192.
  Selected Poems. NDP581.
Rainer Maria Rilke, *Poems from the Book of Hours*.† NDP408.
  Possibility of Being, NDP436.
  Where Silence Reigns. NDP464.
Arthur Rimbaud, *Illuminations*.† NDP56.
  A Season in Hell & The Drunken Boat.† NDP97.
Edouard Roditi, *The Delights of Turkey*. NDP487.
Rodrigo Rey Rosa, *The Good Cripple*. NDP979.
Jerome Rothenberg, *A Book of Witness*. NDP955.
Ralf Rothmann, *Knife Edge*. NDP744.
Nayantara Sahgal, *Mistaken Identity*. NDP742.
Ihara Saikaku, *The Life of an Amorous Woman*. NDP270.
St. John of the Cross. *The Poems of St. John ...* † NDP341.
William Saroyan. *The Daring Young Man ...* NDP852.
Jean-Paul Sartre. *Nausea*. NDP82.
  The Wall (Intimacy). NDP272.
Delmore Schwartz, *In Dreams Begin Responsibilities*. NDP454.
  Screeno: Stories and Poems. NDP985.
Peter Dale Scott, *Coming to Jakarta*, NDP672.
W.G. Sebald, *The Emigrants*. NDP853.
  The Rings of Saturn. NDP881.
  Vertigo. NDP925.
Aharon Shabtai, *J'Accuse*. NDP957.
Hasan Shah, *The Dancing Girl*. NDP777.
Merchant-Prince Shattan, *Manimekhalaï*. NDP674.
Kazuko Shiraishi, *Let Those Who Appear*. NDP940.
C.H. Sisson, *Selected Poems*. NDP826.
Stevie Smith, *Collected Poems*. NDP562.
  Novel on Yellow Paper. NDP778.
Gary Snyder, *Look Out*. NDP949.
  Turtle Island. NDP306.
Gustaf Sobin, *Breaths' Burials*. NDP781.
Muriel Spark, *All the Stories of Muriel Spark*. NDP933.
  The Ghost Stories of Muriel Spark. NDP963.
  Memento Mori. NDP895.
Enid Starkie, *Arthur Rimbaud*. NDP254.
Stendhal, *Three Italian Chronicles*. NDP704.
Antonio Tabucchi, *Pereira Declares*. NDP848.
  Requiem: A Hallucination. NDP944.
Nathaniel Tarn, *Lyrics for the Bride of God*. NDP391.
Emma Tennant, *Strangers: A Family Romance*. NDP960.
Dylan Thomas, *A Child's Christmas in Wales*, NDP972.
  Selected Poems 1934-1952. NDP958.
Tian Wen: A Chinese Book of Origins.† NDP624.
Uwe Timm, *The Invention of Curried Sausage*. NDP854.
Charles Tomlinson, *Selected Poems*. NDP855.
Federico Tozzi, *Love in Vain*. NDP921.
Yuko Tsushima, *The Shooting Gallery*. NDP846.
Leonid Tsypkin, *Summer in Baden-Baden*. NDP962.
Tu Fu, *The Selected Poems*, NDP675.
Niccolò Tucci, *The Rain Came Last*. NDP688.
Dubravka Ugrešić, *The Museum of Unconditional ...* NDP932.
Paul Valéry, *Selected Writings*.† NDP184.
Elio Vittorini, *Conversations in Sicily*. NDP907.
Rosmarie Waldrop, *Blindsight*. NDP971.
Robert Penn Warren, *At Heaven's Gate*. NDP588.
Eliot Weinberger, *Karmic Traces*. NDP908.
Nathanael West, *Miss Lonelyhearts*. NDP125.
Tennessee Williams, *Cat on a Hot Tin Roof*. NDP398.
  The Glass Menagerie. NDP874.
  A Streetcar Named Desire. NDP501.
William Carlos Williams, *Asphodel ...* NDP794.
  Collected Poems: Volumes I & II. NDP730 & NDP731.
  Paterson: Revised Edition, NDP806.
Wisdom Books:
  St. Francis. NDP477.
  Taoists. NDP509.
  The Wisdom of the Desert (Edited by Merton). NDP295.
  Zen Masters. NDP415.

For a complete listing request free catalog from New Directions, 80 Eighth Avenue
New York 10011; or go visit our website, www.ndpublishing.com

†Bilingual